T0146994

Parenting
across the
Life Span

LINDA E. POWERS

PARENTING ACROSS THE LIFE SPAN

iUniverse books may be ordered through booksellers or by contacting:

iUniverse
1663 Liberty Drive
Bloomington, IN 47403
www.iuniverse.com
1-800-Authors (1-800-288-4677)

ISBN: 978-1-5320-5841-7 (sc)
ISBN: 978-1-5320-5840-0 (e)

Library of Congress Control Number: 2018913118

Print information available on the last page.

iUniverse rev. date: 11/14/2018

Contents

Acknowledgments

Understanding the developmental process is an important part of parenting, engaging in positive communication, and maintaining healthy relationships. Watching the developmental process unfold in individuals is fascinating, as each person learns more about himself and the surrounding world. As I observe people of all ages from various walks of life, I find myself wondering things like, "What was it that led this particular person to this career, or this decision?" "Why is this person behaving in a certain way?" "Did an event happen in this person's life which has influenced a level of trust, or impacted the ability to resolve tasks of a certain developmental stage?" For a long time, in the back of my mind, I have entertained the thought of writing a book. I enjoy sharing knowledge and experience with others, and as I pondered the thought more, I realized I could share my knowledge and experience by writing a book intertwining information on the developmental process with my personal and professional experiences.

This book could not have been completed without the support and encouragement of many people. I offer a deep and heartfelt thank you to everyone who has shared in my life's experience, and encouraged my goal of writing this book. My group of faithful proofreaders helped to make my thoughts a reality. They have patiently read, re-read, edited, offered suggestions, and asked necessary questions at times, all leading to the finished product.

Special thanks to Kala, who read my manuscript and offered words of encouragement. Her professional wisdom, calmness, and ethical practice have inspired me. I value Kala's professional knowledge and experience, and I relied on her guidance to insure expression of information on various stages of development. Thank you, Kala, for taking the time out of your busy life to support my endeavor.

To Lois, my dear friend and former colleague in the mental health profession, who patiently read chapter by chapter, offering thoughts, suggestions, and questions, a big thank you for your encouragement and patience. The continual support of friends is crucial to a project, and I sincerely appreciate your ongoing support. Your thoughts and questions served an important purpose as I reflected on my writing.

Glenn, my former boss, served as a supportive reader throughout the process, offering his insight from years of clinical and administrative experience in the mental health field. Over the years, Glenn and I have had many discussions on the contributions made by Erik Erikson and others, and I knew I could rely on him to offer suggestions and give his perspective on the strengths of my book, as well as pose questions about certain areas. Thank you, Glenn.

Jon patiently edited and re-edited my manuscript, offering suggestions, ideas, and questions. Everyone who knows me is aware that I am technologically challenged, and Jon's patient supportiveness helped me survive computer glitches I encountered along the way. Throughout the process, Jon and I had several discussions about chapter titles. As a reader, Jon provided a different perspective. He is not in my profession and he is not a parent, but his IT experience, broad base knowledge, and the objective experience he has gained working with children, provided feedback from another perspective. Thank you, Jon, for your thoughts and ideas, as well as your patience.

Digitalizing photos was a task I didn't look forward to. My thanks and appreciation to Conrad, who helped me accomplish this task. Thanks to Jon for his assistance in that area, also.

Professor Joshua Dallaire, an adjunct professor of English at Manchester Community College, SNHU, and Granite State College, provided a final editing. Thank you, Josh, for your suggestions and help. Having an English professor edit my manuscript before submitting it to the publisher raised my confidence level.

In graduate school, Heather (Ramer) Souther and I collaborated on a project entitled *Parenting the Preschool Child*. My thanks to Heather for granting permission for me to utilize information from that project in the book.

Thank you to iuniverse publishing company for guidance and assistance in helping this project become a reality.

In acknowledging contributors, I feel indebted to all the researchers, educators, professionals, psychologists, psychiatrists, and others, who have gone before us and laid the foundation for understanding the process of human development. My gratefulness includes appreciation for the work, insight, and observations of current research and the information that is shared. Continued work and knowledge provide motivation for us to continue to learn and deepen our understanding.

And, finally, thank you to all who supported my idea and my work. Thank you to all who have shown interest. I hope you find this to be an enlightening journey.

Dedication

This book is dedicated to my daughters, Rebecca, Jennifer, and Cathryn, who have been my companions on my personal parenting journey. You have blessed my life with love, pride, and joy. The frustrations and challenges have served as important learning tools for all of us.

To my grandchildren: Spencer, Allison, Benjamin, Ethan, and Cooper. You are the lights of my life. Sharing your lives, and watching you grow as you develop into caring and responsible individuals is one of my greatest pleasures.

Introduction

Parenting: A Path in the Journey of Life

The path of parenting takes many twists and turns as we invest our energy into nurturing others. There are many wonderful surprises and proud moments along the path, interspersed with times of intense worry, sadness, frustration, and disappointment. As a mom of three daughters, I experienced the parenting journey firsthand, and I learned a lot through the years. Like all families, our family has had its ups and downs, and as I reflect on the years and experiences, it is hard for me to believe the journey began more than forty years ago. My children's births sometimes feel like they were only days ago. It seems like only yesterday my husband and I were reading bedtime stories and tucking in little ones, then chauffeuring them to swim, dance, music lessons, sports, and social activities. The busy, chaotic years are past, and I now experience the rewards of being a grandmother to five great kids! Memories and reflections—where did the time go?

I also experienced parenting through the eyes of others, as my career provided me with the chance to learn how society and culture influence parenting. As a child and adolescent psychotherapist, an educator, and a former pediatric nurse, I have had the opportunity to assist other parents in understanding the developmental process and parenting.

We are constantly faced with challenges and stressors. It is often easier to deal with stressful events if we understand what is happening. Parenting can be a more positive experience if we understand the developmental process, have good communication tools, and use effective strategies to manage stress while spending quality time with our families. My purpose in writing this book is to strengthen our understanding as we nurture future generations and ourselves.

Parenting as a Career

Parenting is one of the many great privileges we have. The unconditional love, joy, and pride that accompany parenting are profound and deep. Along with these come enormous responsibilities, times of worry, frustration, anger, sadness, heartache, disappointment, and sometimes exhaustion. When we are parents, we are on call 24-7, with little or no time off. Even when we have a day off, or a vacation, our thoughts of the children are ever present: *Are they okay? Are they safe? How is the day going for them?* As parents, we often second-guess ourselves. *Did I make the right decision? Did I handle that situation appropriately?*

Many careers are defined as providing a service, and in parenting, we perform a great service—shaping the lives of future generations. Parenting is an ongoing lifetime commitment and one of the greatest challenges we undertake. I think of parenting as a career, one we never retire from. In our careers, we invest time and energy, with the goal of performing our jobs well and being rewarded with a paycheck. We look forward to the paycheck to provide housing, food, and the necessities for our families, and maybe some extras. After investing many years in our careers, we retire and receive benefits packages. We also invest tremendous energy and time parenting our children. The constant responsibility for someone else's well being can be overwhelming. Although we do not receive monetary compensation for parenting, we derive many benefits. The rewards from parenting include the pride when our children succeed, the gratitude when our children recover from illness, the relief when our children are spared injuries, and the love we feel when our children do or say something that melts our hearts. These intangible rewards eclipse monetary rewards and outweigh the difficulties that visit all families. Investing our all in our children, we hope we are doing a good job and that our children will be happy and successful. As parents, we will always worry, whether we admit it or not.

Usually, when we begin a job, we participate in an orientation and are given guidelines to follow; expectations are clearly stated, and we are accountable to our superiors. Our performance is periodically assessed. When we become parents, there is no formal training to prepare us. The only training we have is how we were parented—what we observed, learned, and experienced. Perhaps we babysat, had younger siblings, or worked with children in community settings and learned through those experiences. But are we prepared for the intense 24-7 demands of being responsible for a human being who is totally dependent on us? If we stop to consider the daunting responsibility of raising this child and providing nurturance, guidance, and modeling, we may wonder, *How can I do this?* As time passes, we get to know our child; we begin to feel more comfortable in the parenting role, and it feels less scary.

The demands, concerns, and nature of the relationships change as children grow. Just as we have goals in our careers, we have goals in parenting. The overall goal of parenting is to raise a responsible, productive adult who can be autonomous, function as an individual within the guidelines of society, and have healthy relationships. When we hold that sweet, helpless newborn in our arms, however, the last thing on our minds is the long-term goal of parenting. We are so overcome with awe and love, not to mention exhaustion and perhaps fear, we wonder, *Will I be a good parent?* We just know we want the best for our child.

As the child matures into adulthood, we invest less time and energy, but we are still parents, and we are there for our children in different ways. Through experience, we learn that we need to keep some of our thoughts and advice to ourselves. With instant communication at our fingertips, how many of us have attempted to reach our adult children, only to have them not answer because they're involved in something? But what happens if an adult child attempts to reach a parent and the parent doesn't answer? After two or three attempts, the child might start to worry about the parent, and when the parent is finally reached, the adult child might say, "Where have you been? What are you doing? Why didn't you answer the phone?"

Parenting does not end when our children reach a certain age. We may have less control and fewer responsibilities, and the ways of communicating are different, but our role as parent is always there. When they are adults, our children need us in different ways. For example, our nineteen-year-old is away at college, facing the world bravely, confident she can face all the twists and turns in her journey of life. Suddenly, she is feeling overwhelmed and less confident, so she calls home, not sure what she wants. If we attempt to give her direct advice, she may resist because she thinks of herself as having all the answers. She doesn't want advice, so we ask ourselves, *What does she need?* We need to tread lightly.

I realized this late one night when my daughter called, overwhelmed with her schedule during her sophomore year in college. Having been awoken from a sound sleep, I listened to her and responded with suggestions for time management. Wrong response! She felt that I didn't understand the stress of academia. I reminded her that I went back to grad school at the age of fifty. She then reminded me that my experience of attending grad school as a middle-aged adult could not be compared to a nineteen-year-old's experience. I countered with a reminder that when I was nineteen, I was a student in a three-year nursing program affiliated with a hospital, and many mornings I was up at five thirty, worked on the floors for several hours, and then attended class for several hours. Again, a bad response. She said, "Mom, you just don't get it!" No, I guess I didn't. I was too quick (and half-asleep) to realize I should have listened and validated.

Parenting is not restricted to only those adults who raise their own children. Many serve as parents, or parental figures, to children other than their own. We use our skills of caring, managing, and advocating for others, and through all the demands, we must take care of ourselves. The word *parent*, in the verb form, means to care for, provide for, protect, or oversee. We all must parent ourselves, in the sense that it is important to care for ourselves, nurture ourselves, and oversee our well being. We do this in the form of rest, relaxation, or a fun activity. We need to remember we are humans, not machines capable of functioning at full capacity all the time. It is easy to say, "I'll do one more thing, and then I will stop." So often, that one thing turns into numerous other things we feel we should do. We forget to prioritize. We all need to identify our limits and know when to slow down. Some people reward themselves with an activity or a token; others find that exercise or yoga revitalizes them. I often reward myself with reading a good book, drinking a cup of tea, or practicing yoga. Chocolate is always a reward too!

Throughout our parenting careers, it is important for us to remember that we have a learning curve. No one has all the answers, and we all make mistakes. We will continue to grow throughout the journey, and we can learn from our errors. As our children grow and learn, we also continue to grow and learn.

Healthy Interdependence Is the Long-Term Goal of Parenting

We expect adults to be independent in terms of thinking for themselves and taking care of their needs while living within the community and its guidelines, as well as participating in relationships with family members, friends, neighbors, peers, and colleagues. Although we strive for independence, no one can be totally independent. At some point, we all need other people. We are in multiple relationships throughout our lives, and if those relationships are healthy, we function *interdependently*, meaning we try to maintain a balance on the continuum between total dependence and total independence. We can be autonomous with our thoughts and feelings and at the same time rely on others in a healthy way.

Our position on the spectrum between dependence and independence will vary, but as healthy adults, we are never totally dependent or totally independent. If we are to be successful as individuals and in relationships, *interdependence* is important. We all rely on others, whether it is a spouse or partner to share household chores, errands, and life experiences with, or reliance among family members to share responsibilities. The person who lives alone relies on others for support, friendship, and love. We may enjoy the companionship of a friend when we shop. We rely on teachers to educate and medical professionals to meet our health needs. We all need stores, farms, and community resources. We all need others at different times, and the trick is helping our children learn about healthy interdependence. Emotional interdependence helps us maintain a balance through a strong support system. Interdependence is ever present in the work environment when we work as teams. Understanding development through the life cycle aids us in relationships, whether the relationship is family, work related, or social.

Newborn infants begin the journey of life as totally dependent, relying on parents and caregivers to meet all their needs. As infants grow and develop life skills, they gradually become less dependent. Parents and adults continue to provide guidance as children mature into adulthood. If we become grandparents, new experiences and paths to learning emerge. Although we don't have the full time responsibility, our children and grandchildren remain part of our lives, and while the concerns may be somewhat different, we continue to be there when we can. So, no, we never retire.

Parenting Ourselves and Others

We continue to take care of ourselves and provide support and nurturance for others. Not only are we strong role models for our own children and adolescents, but we may also be in situations where we are surrogate parents for someone else's children. Perhaps a young adult is a surrogate parent for her younger sibling. Or maybe other adult family members assume the role of surrogate parents. At these times, it is helpful to understand the developmental process through a life span. In the mid-twentieth century, Erik Erikson, a researcher of social and emotional development, identified eight stages of social and emotional development that occur during the life cycle, which will be addressed in the chapters that follow.

Some of us have had the experience of parenting our parents, as they have aged and are less independent. Those of us who have been in that situation know how frustrating and challenging it can be. I found parenting my own children easier than parenting my mother. When our parents become frail and vulnerable, roles may be reversed, and we become their caretakers. Perhaps it is providing physical assistance, driving them to a destination, or helping them walk. Maybe our parent is experiencing dementia and we need to be responsible for overseeing medical decisions, everyday care, and financial decisions. I found the role reversal to be both unsettling and enlightening. In her eighties, my mom, who was always a source of strength and guidance, became unable to safely care for herself and make her own decisions. She needed someone to guide her decisions and supervise her care. She needed someone to be strong for her. At that time, my daughters were grown. I had been used to parenting my own offspring, and now, suddenly, I was parenting the person who had parented me. It was a profound learning experience.

At some point in our adult lives, we realize the importance of caring for ourselves. We have others who support us, but we must nurture and care for ourselves to stay healthy. It is up to each of us to set our boundary of when and how to parent ourselves. Nurturing yourself might include being able to say no to some of the requests from others, or our own long lists of "*I should.*" It might be scheduling a rest time or a centering time in the midst of a busy day. A brief meditation or a walk outside to catch a glimpse of nature can help us gain perspective and contributes to self-care. Maintaining self-care and our health may require balancing many responsibilities, but parenting ourselves is important. We have heard the saying "You can't take care of someone else if you don't take care of yourself." We cannot be of help and value to others if we are exhausted and stressed.

Through our experiences in adulthood, as we parent others and ourselves, we continue learning. In adulthood, as long as we are open to learning, we will enrich our social and emotional skills and deepen our spiritual growth. As we experience life, we become more aware of the importance of moral and ethical development, and our own emotional growth leads to wisdom and patience.

Chapter 1

A Brief History of Human Development Theories

Growth and Development

Development can be defined as the process of growth to reach maturity through progressive and sequential attainment of skills. In other words, development is similar to climbing a flight of stairs; you place your foot solidly on one stair before you go to the next stair. It is the same with development; a child must reach certain stages before going on to the next stage. Understanding the developmental process is key to parenting. Knowing what is expected at different stages helps us maintain consistency and a nurturing environment. Understanding our children and knowing what is expected at certain ages makes parenting easier.

We seek guidance from pediatricians, educators, psychologists, counselors, friends, books, and other parents for the best way to raise our children. Sometimes the information can be overwhelming, and it is often conflicting. Parenting styles have changed through the generations, and it can be tiring to continually hear older generations remind us of "back in my day."

In our contemporary world, there are many variations of parenting, and that can leave parents feeling confused or doubting their own parenting style. I believe parents instinctively know their child, and as parents, the best we can do is consider the recommendations, assess the situation, and make the best decision for our child at a given moment. At the same time, we have to be mindful that past generations have turned out okay, so maybe there is something of value in what the older generation is saying. Some parents find it works to incorporate a little of the old while acknowledging contemporary times and current understanding of development. I believe *respect* is one very important thing that can be learned from past generations and should be encouraged in future generations.

Many theories have evolved over the years, enriching our understanding of human development. My learning and experience have led me to believe that the foundation began to grow with theorists like Erik Erikson and Jean Piaget. Others have influenced my thinking along the way, and we continue to learn from contemporary theorists and researchers. The list of references at the end of the book also serves as a source of information.

Development is an amazing process, some of which happens on its own. Growth and development are not restricted to physical growth alone. While we cannot control the hereditary part of the developmental process, we can influence the environment our children grow up in. A supportive environment nurtures the emotional, cognitive, moral, spiritual, and social aspects of development. Through encouragement, we can nurture children's gifts and talents and expose them to opportunities that will expand growth in all areas. We can provide nurturance and as much consistency as life allows. We can help our children be wise decision-makers, industrious workers, and kind, committed, respectful individuals.

Each child develops at an individual rate, and the range of development that is considered normal and appropriate varies. Some children may develop earlier in one area and later in another. For example, at the age of three, one child might display the language ability of a four-year-old and fine motor skills of a three-year-old. Another three-year-old child might have the gross motor skills of a four-year-old but the language skills of a two-and-a-half-year old. Children within the same family can develop at different rates and still be considered within the normal range. Pediatricians monitor development at well-child visits and can address any parental concerns.

Children will regress, or return to an earlier behavioral stage, with increased anxiety, a change in routine, fatigue, or other stressors. Slight regression is temporary and considered within the norm. A child might regress in one area only, maintaining the levels of development in other areas. For example, a three-year-old child might react to a new sibling by showing more dependence on his mother, but he maintains his levels of motor, speech/language, and cognitive development. Or an eighteen-month-old, picking up on stress within the family, may temporarily refuse to eat independently, while continuing to progress in other areas of development. A six-year-old might respond to anxiety with increased whining. I find the best way to address a period of regression is to meet the child halfway. If a parent gives in to the behavior, the period of regression may last longer. If a parent approaches the child in a manner that is too stern, the child may not feel validated, and symptoms could continue longer. When responding to the three-year-old who regresses after the arrival of a new sibling, it is helpful if the parent carves out small periods of one-on-one time for the parent and child. It doesn't hurt to casually comment now and then about what a big help the child is and how proud you are of him This way, the child feels validated, loved, and appreciated. If a parent gives in and impatiently feeds the eighteen-month-old all the time, the child may not regain the previous stage of independent eating without a battle. If a parent meets the child halfway, making a game by doing some of the feeding, alternating with encouraging the child to feed herself, the child may be more likely to resume eating independently. If, as a parent, you are concerned because the regressive stage seems to be lasting longer than you think it should, or is getting more intense, address it with your pediatrician or other developmental professional.

Children may not verbalize anxieties, but they do experience anxiety and worries, which are expressed in their behaviors. Some of these common behaviors are thumb sucking, hair twirling, stuttering, nail biting, throat clearing, or eye blinking. We refer to these as *tensional outlets*. Many tensional outlets are considered normal and are often associated with certain stages of development. Your pediatrician can monitor your child's development and recommend strategies as needed, or interventions if required.

A healthy person is often referred to as a "whole" or "unified" person. Think of a whole person encompassing physical, emotional, cognitive, social, language, spiritual, moral, and sexual areas of development. All areas develop simultaneously, at individual rates, and integrate to form a unique person. For example, infants cannot lift their heads until they reach a certain level of development. Children cannot interact with others if they do not have the opportunity of exposure to varied and appropriate social situations. Speech does not occur until sufficient cognitive, physical, social, and emotional developmental levels are reached.

Personality and Temperament

Both heredity and the environment influence development and personality. With the integration of the neurological, motor, and sensory systems, and the cooperation of cognitive and emotional systems, the different areas of development merge, and a new developmental level is attained, contributing to the formation of personality.

When we say, "He has a great personality," what do we mean? What is it that we like about this person? Is it because he is a good communicator? He makes us feel good? Could it be that he tells great jokes? Is he a good listener and always has time for someone else? Is it because he is caring and compassionate? He has lots of energy? Is he genuine? Do we find his work ethic admirable? What is it?

How do we define *personality*? This question has been asked millions of times, and various people have defined *personality* and offered different theories with many variations. For example, *Americana Dictionary* defines personality as "the combination of characteristics, or qualities that form an individual's distinctive character;" (synonyms listed are: "character, nature, disposition, temperament, makeup, persona, psyche)." The definition listed on Dictionary.com is "the visible aspects of one's character as it impresses others." *Merriam-Webster's* statement is the following: "1) quality or state of being a person; 2) complex of characteristics that distinguishes an individual; the totality of an individual's behavioral and emotional characteristics." The *Kids' Encyclopedia Britannica* states that personality is the "whole collection of individual thoughts and emotions and behaviors that make a person different from another." The *American Psychological Association Dictionary* defines personality as "1) individual differences in characteristic patterns of thinking, feeling and behaving. Differences in personality: sociability, irritability; 2) the understanding of how various characteristics of a person come together as a whole."

There are many definitions of personality. If we read them all, they present the same concepts, but are the definitions all-inclusive? Which one do you think best describes the word personality? My definition of personality is:

> The behavior patterns of a person through the development of the unique and collective characteristics, attitudes, beliefs, thoughts, emotions, and behaviors of an individual, influenced by past experiences and the present, with the interacting effects of heredity and the environment (including family environment, society, culture, peers, and experiences). These patterns remain relatively consistent and stable throughout time.

This definition addresses the uniqueness of each individual yet takes into account how past experiences may have influenced the person. It considers the hereditary influence, along with the person's current situations. This concept of personality encompasses how personality traits develop, while remaining persistent over time.

When we talk about personality, we need to consider temperament. Dr. T. Berry Brazelton, a well-known pediatrician who practiced in Cambridge, Massachusetts, discusses temperament in children and offers insight into the emotional and social development of infants and young children. Dr. Brazelton has addressed the different areas of development in his books, lectures, and practice. He acknowledges the uniqueness of each individual and offers parenting advice. In his books *Touchpoints: The Essential Reference to Your Child's Emotional and Behavioral Development* (1992) and *Touchpoints: Three to Six: Your Child's Emotional and Behavioral Development* (2001), Dr.

Brazelton advises that temperament is part of personality, and he explains how the stages of development can be impacted by a child's temperament.

Dr. Brazelton identified three types of temperament: (1) quiet, (2) average, and (3) active/hypersensitive. The *quiet* child tends to be introspective. She is observant and may not show an immediate behavioral response. In fact, other than her eyes watching everything, it may appear as if she is not involved, but she is really taking it all in. She is internalizing and processing what she has seen, heard, and felt.

The *active*, or *hypersensitive*, child is easily stimulated and has difficulty shutting out distractions or selecting appropriate stimuli to respond to. The brain has neurotransmitters, or messengers, that transmit signals. Evidence has indicated that in the hyperactive child, neurotransmitters in the brain transmit many signals without screening them. In contrast, the brain of a quiet, or less active, child is able to shut out some of the distractions or stimuli.

The hyperactive or hypersensitive child is physically active, always on the move, and is often kinesthetic, needing to touch everything to get a sense of what it is. His sense of touch at times seems overactive as he seems to need to experience learning by touching and trying everything. He is very reactive and also sensitive. He may show emotions readily and emotions are often overly exaggerated. This child needs quiet periods with decreased stimulation to put himself back together.

The child of *average* temperament is somewhere in the middle and experiences learning through both astute observation and touching/sensing, with more balance. Dr.

Brazelton and others who have studied the behavior of young children have observed that a child's temperament determines responses to the environment. Understanding your child's temperament is helpful in structuring the environment and in communication with your child.

Touchpoints

Dr. Brazelton identifies *touchpoints* as "those predictable times that occur just before a surge of rapid growth in any line of development" (Brazelton 1992, xvii). Touchpoints are recognized as important markers in the developmental process and may be accompanied by regressions and spurts. Dr. Brazelton points out in his book *Touchpoints: The Essential Reference to Your Child's Emotional and Behavioral Development* (1992) that for this short period, a child's behavior falls apart. These times are recognized to be universal; no one is exempt. It may seem like the responses are more exaggerated at times in some children, while on the other hand, some children seem to flow through the stages with less upheaval. In the introduction to his book *Touchpoints* (1992), Dr. Brazelton refers to his map of behavioral and emotional development of early childhood to "help parents navigate the predictable spurts in development and the equally predictable issues that they raise in all families" (Brazelton 1992, xvii). His description follows: "Unlike yardsticks of physical development, this map has several dimensions. Psychological growth takes place in many directions, and not all at once. The cost of each new achievement can temporarily disrupt the child's—and even the whole family's progress" (Brazelton 1992, xvii).

Dr. Brazelton encourages using touchpoints as a time to teach parents and caregivers about normal development, behavior, and variations. He recommends developmentally appropriate intervention strategies that encourage healthy development and ways to minimize stress. Although Dr. Brazelton's map only goes through the stages of early childhood, there are critical times throughout the life span that trigger regression and confusion. As mentioned previously, regression to a certain degree is normal and can be expected with any change, stressor, fatigue, or illness. Regression may not be obvious to others during daily routines. As adults, we may regress in certain areas when we have a major change, stressor, illness, or loss. Maybe it is slight and not noticeable to others, because we continue to appear to function at our usual level. But we may notice the change within ourselves as we feel more tired, less patient, or crave comfort foods and favorite activities. No one is exempt, because as humans we are capable of a wide range of emotions, tempered in varying degrees with logic and reasoning, and we all respond to our environment depending on who we are.

Touchpoint times during the first six years:

1. Pregnancy
2. The newborn individual
3. The newborn parents
4. Three weeks

5. Six to eight weeks
6. Four months
7. Seven months
8. Nine months
9. One year
10. Fifteen months
11. Eighteen months
12. Two years
13. Three years
14. Four years
15. Five years
16. Six years

(Brazelton 1992)

Erik Erikson's Theory of Social and Emotional Development

Erikson began studying under Sigmund Freud, and like others in his time, Erikson realized that Freud's psychoanalytic theories did not give adequate consideration to social, emotional, and cognitive development. Erikson studied people of all ages and cultures, including residents of Native American reservations. As his observations of children's play and communication motivated him, he was one of the first to acknowledge the importance of play in the young child. Over the years, he formulated his psychosocial theory of development across the life span. At the request of the National Institute of Mental Health, Erikson contributed to the three-volume work *The Course of*

Life, Psychoanalytical Contributions Toward Understanding Personality Development (Erikson 1980), which later became *The Life Cycle Completed—A Review* (1982). In his dissertation, Erikson explained the history of his developing interest, based on the idea that things other than instincts influence people. He mentioned that the timing of this theory was appropriate, believing that people were historically, technologically, culturally, and psychologically ready for the expansion of the psychoanalytic theory. In his writings, Erikson maintained that Freud's psychoanalytic theory, although limited, provided a basis for his own interest in the development of a child. He credited Freud's work as a foundation for future theories. He credited others, including Anna Freud (Sigmund Freud's daughter) and Heinz Hartmann, as contributing to his own study of ego development, citing Anna Freud's statement, "We need to look to the accidental environmental influences" (Erikson 1982, 19). He considered the statement of H. Hartman, "There were many additional problems of ego growth and ego functioning which needed consideration," (Erikson 1982, 16) as influential in the foundation of his own theory.

Erikson's psychosocial theory correlates the emotional, psychological, cognitive, and social aspects of development through the life span, with the impact of social, cultural, and familial influences on personality development. According to Erikson's theory, development is sequential, with all developmental stages being interdependent. The theory creates a picture of a healthy, integrated person who can function in the world as a self-aware individual, and also interact in positive ways with other people. Through

Erikson's developmental model, a person's emotional-social identity develops out of graded integrations. In *Childhood and Society* (1963), Erikson advised that as parents develop with their children, they face a constant challenge, especially if there is more than one child in the family. To paraphrase Erikson, the family brings up a baby, who is also controlling the family. Erikson's work also increased the awareness that play and work are not mutually exclusive (Erikson 1963).

Over the past thirty to forty years, Erikson's theory has created controversy, as some theorists believe that the theory was primarily based on white, middle-class males. Feminist theorists have expressed that Erikson's theory does not adequately address the stages of *identity* and *intimacy* in the female. Many theorists believe Erikson's chart should be reworked to balance these stages in males and females. Many people, myself included, believe that Erikson's stages provide a strong guideline for emotional-social development through the lifetime, and individual variations can be acknowledged. However, as pointed out by Judith Horst in 1995, Erikson "is credited for asserting that women are different, not inferior or deviant, from men, and their ability to connect and relate to others adds unique perspectives, adding a female perspective to vision and creativity in the workplace" (Horst 1995, 273). Erikson's original works were complex, and we are reminded by several professional sources that Erikson never intended a controversy. An important focus in Erikson's beliefs is the weaving of interpersonal relationships throughout developmental stages.

Erikson's theory provides a guideline for the

developmental stages throughout life, and its flexibility allows for adaptation according to individual development. Identity is a stage we revisit many times throughout our lives. Mary Catherine Bateson, who was a teaching assistant to Erikson during part of his professorship at Harvard, states: "The Eriksonian model is best known for its description of the identity crisis of early adulthood, yet the real landmarks are not crises but the development of strengths" (Bateson 2011, 66).

Bateson (2011) further supports the Eriksonian theory by advising that we revisit the stages of development throughout our lives. She states:

> The aspects of Erikson's work that seems to have been least integrated into general understanding is that the central developmental challenge of each stage reappears or is anticipated in every other stage. Thus, the crisis of identity in youth is anticipated in every step of individuation and autonomy from birth on, and must be revisited at every later stage. That which is first represented at birth by physical separation from the mother is played out as differentiation and later on, in new forms of autonomy and a search for continuity, so that in old age we ask not "Who am I" but "Am I still the person I have spent a lifetime becoming?" (Bateson 2011, 66–67)

Erikson's theory promotes *interdependence* as a part of healthy functioning. In *Childhood and Society* (1963), he acknowledges culture's influence on developmental expectations, and he mentions in his observations that play is often different between the genders, partially because of cultural expectations.

Erikson's theory can be described as hierarchical in that the developmental stages are like steps; one must attain a certain level of mastering before progressing on to the next. However, one does not have to completely master one stage to move on to the next. Although sequential, Erikson's stages are fluid in that they allow a person to go back to revisit a stage previously attained, as life's circumstances dictate. One stage that I believe we all revisit time and again is *identity*. Through our journeys, we encounter many changes, and sometimes those changes necessitate revisiting our identity. For example, a woman may be established in her career and in her relationships, and she sees herself as multidimensional; as a worker, friend, spouse, or partner. She becomes a parent. Now she is also identified as someone's mom. The years of parenting contribute to a strong sense of identity as a mom, and suddenly there is the empty nest, and her identity needs adjusting. She will always be a mom but now in a different light. When she retires from her full-time career, she will need to revisit her identity again. In the meantime, grandchildren may have arrived, adding yet another dimension to her identity. Then, finally, the wise and mature years descend upon her (I prefer the description "wise and mature" to elderly), and she must revisit her identity again when she needs to depend more and more on others as she becomes frail.

Erikson stressed that interdependence of systems is crucial in the developmental process to lead to a healthy, whole person who is integrated. He viewed a "whole" person as one who can find a comfortable balance between work and play; a balance between being autonomous and in relationships with others, maintaining clear boundaries, and a balance between family or intimate relationships and relationships with others in the community. Erikson's beliefs also included the importance of blending medicine and health of the physical body with mental health.

Erikson's theory also describes the three processes of organization within human beings. These processes are the *soma*, the *psyche* or *emotional* process, and the *ethos*. Soma is the biological process of the organ systems and covers the physical aspect of development. The psyche, or emotional, process is related to the emotional development of the individual. Ethos is the communal process of cultural development within society and addresses interdependence, an important part of an emotionally healthy life (Erikson 1982).

Erikson has described the psychosocial crises, basic strengths, negative aspects, principles of social order, and ritualizations of each stage and how the attainment of each stage, or lack of attainment, impacts healthy development. With each stage, he clearly identifies the strength of accomplishing a developmental task, versus a negative aspect of not reaching a certain level of attainment. We will go into a little more detail on individual development of different stages in the following chapters.

Jean Piaget, who identified theories concerning stages of cognitive development, stated, "The great merit of Erikson's stages … is precisely that he attempted, by situating the Freudian mechanisms with more general types of conduct (working, exploring, etc.) to postulate the integration of previous acquisitions at subsequent levels" (Erikson 1982, 76).

The general outline of Erikson's theory is below (Erikson 1982).

Stage	Strength achieved from accomplishing the developmental task	Versus	Negative characteristic from not attaining a successful level of attainment
Infancy	Basic Trust		Basic mistrust
Toddler	Autonomy		Shame and Doubt
Preschool	Initiative		Guilt
School age	Industry		Inferiority
Adolescence	Identity		Identity Confusion
Young Adulthood	Intimacy		Isolation
Adulthood	Generativity		Stagnation
Older Adulthood	Integrity		Despair

Adler's Humanistic Theory of Personality Development

Dr. Alfred Adler, a psychiatrist who branched his humanistic theory off Freud's original psychoanalytic theory, contributed much to the understanding of personality and development. Adler believed in the unified, or whole, person, who is an individual yet simultaneously functions in relationships and society. Like Erikson, Adler believed in the importance of relationships and social exposure in the process of development. He stressed the importance of family and parents being educated in the developmental process. He strongly believed that the family sets the example of the first social interactions for a child. He was a proponent of the birth order theory, which proposes that a child's placement in the family contributes to certain characteristics. He believed that traits, or characteristics, are consistent throughout life, and an individual usually follows a consistent lifestyle. Adler was also an advocate for education being a positive experience. Adler was establishing his theories as the *object relations* theorists were beginning, and Adler's research served as an inspiration to many future researchers in the area of personality development.

Object Relations Theories

One cannot delve into the history of human development theories without touching upon the object relations theories. Object relations developed as a variation of Freud's psychoanalytic theory as psychologists and those who studied child development realized the importance of relationships in social and emotional development. The theory was based on observations that humans are primarily motivated by a need for contact with others and the primary need for relationships.

Some of the people who contributed to the object relations theory are R. Fairbirn, Melanie Klein, Anna Freud, Donald Winnicott, Heinz Hartmann, Otto Kernberg, Heinz Kohut, Edith Jacobson, and Margaret Mahler. Each of them studied the process of an infant moving from dependency on the mother figure to individuation during the first three years of life. The word *object* refers to a significant person who satisfies the infant's needs and becomes the recipient of the infant's affections.

All of the object relations theorists provided interpretations of the relationship between mother and child. For example, Margaret Mahler focused on individuation by identifying stages that an infant goes through in practicing to break away from the mother. One of Dr. Winnicott's contributions was the significance of a transitional object in a young child's life as the child is learning to separate. Dr. Winnicott, a pediatrician, approached this from both the psychological and physical developmental areas.

Contributions from Other Theorists

As Erikson continued to expand on his theory of social and emotional development through the life span, many other contributions on child development were made. In the 1920s, and again in the 1950s with B.F. Skinner's operant conditioning, attention was drawn to behaviorism.

Arnold Gesell and his team at the Gesell Institute made major contributions to understanding child development, and they continue to be a resource today (Gesell et al. 1955).

Dr. Benjamin Spock became a household name, in the 1940s and 1950s with his contributions on parenting, nurturing, and the role of structure. Dr. Hiam Ginott became well known in the mid-twentieth century with his books and guidance on parent-child relationships and communication between parents and children. Dr. Rudolf Dreikurs, a follower of Alfred Adler, was a pioneer in the movement for parent education groups in the 1950s and 1960s. In the 1970s and 1980s, we saw parent education trainings like Parent Effectiveness Training, Active Parenting, and Systematic Training for Effective Parenting (STEP).

Many others, like Dr. Fitzhugh Dodson and Dr. James Dobson, have made contributions to help parents understand and communicate with their children. Harvard University has had an ongoing preschool project centered on development of the young child. Dr. Burton White, who headed the Harvard research project on development in the 1970s, has been associated with many developments in understanding the infant, toddler, and young child. Today, Dr. Daniel Siegel is the author of books on discipline and communication between parents and children.

Multiple researchers in child development, including psychologists, pediatricians, psychiatrists, educators, and others, continue to promote healthy family functioning and guidance to parents and those who work with children. Ongoing research shows us that adverse childhood experiences (ACE), such as trauma or abuse, can impact both the physical and mental health of children and adults. The New Hampshire Children's Trust Fund, located in Concord NH, offers ongoing education and support, with the goal of preventing child abuse and neglect.

As time goes on, ideas and recommendations for child-rearing change, as a review of the last hundred years shows us. What is right? What is the best way? As a parent or care provider, one can learn about recommendations and make decisions based on logic and instinct. I believe, most times, parents know what is best for their child.

Piaget's Cognitive Theory

While Erikson was promoting his theory, Jean Piaget formed his cognitive theories of early-childhood development. Piaget's theory has been considered one of the most influential, as it addresses learning from the perspectives of neuroscience and psychology. It focuses on a child's development in terms of processing information, development of perceptual skills, language learning, and other aspects of brain development. Piaget identified four stages of cognitive development: *sensorimotor, preoperational, concrete operational,* and *formal operational.*

Sensorimotor, the first stage, occurs from birth to about eighteen to twenty-four months, when infants and toddlers learn through their senses: feeling, touching, sucking, seeing, and hearing. They discover themselves and the relationships between their bodies and the environment.

The preoperational stage, which usually occurs between

ages two to seven years, starts when the child begins to talk. We see rapid increase in language skills during this period. During this stage, a child experiences life through play and often pretends, using an object to represent something else. Preschool children engage in symbolic play and mimic others. Parallel play, when children play alongside each other, is very common in young children. As their social skills develop, parallel play decreases as interaction skills become stronger.

The concrete operational stage occurs around ages seven to twelve. During this stage, children show evidence of thinking logically and concretely. As they approach the last stage, the formal operational stage, hypothetical thinking and abstract reasoning skills begin to develop. The formal operational stage begins in adolescence and continues through adulthood. Over the years, many have compared Erikson's stages of emotional-social development to Piaget's stages of cognitive development.

Social Learning Theory

We know that children learn by example. Children are constantly observing the adults and teens in their lives, and children are role models for other children. While parents play significant roles as models for their children, other adults also provide strong examples and are powerful mentors for youth. Every day, children and teens observe the actions of adults who are not their own parents, such as caregivers, teachers, family members, family friends, neighbors, and celebrities. As they approach adolescence, youth may choose, either unconsciously or consciously, a person who will serve as their mentor in career choices and future lifestyles.

Albert Bandura, a psychologist in the twentieth century, studied the social aspect of learning. In 1977, Bandura published a module entitled Social Learning Theory, which is also known as the Social Cognitive Theory. This theory addresses the social and psychological principles that influence behavior. Bandura acknowledged five stages of observable behavior:

1. Paying attention
2. Remembering observations
3. Reproducing actions
4. Becoming motivated to reproduce what is observed
5. Perfecting and imitating what is observed
   (Rykman 1993; Hjelle and Ziegler 1992)

Prior to the work of Bandura and other social learning theorists, behaviorists advocated that behavior is learned in response to direct stimulus, and reinforcement increases the likelihood that the behavior will be repeated. Behaviorists did not acknowledge the involvement of cognition in the process. The research of Julian Rotter, a contemporary of Bandura's, provided parallel findings that ongoing interaction between behavior, cognition, and the environment occurs with learning.

Many people have likened the social learning theory to a bridge between behavioral and cognitive learning theories because it encompasses attention, memory, observation, and motivation. The research of Bandura, Rotter, and others has shown that through the complex process of integration of environmental influences, observing the behavior and consequences of that behavior, and the internal cognitive process, learning is enhanced with reinforcement.

Over the years, research has continued to show that people, especially children, learn through modeling. It is also known that consequences are considered in the cognition process, and positive reinforcement of behavior encourages a person to continue that behavior. Throughout the process of understanding child development, some ideas have been cast aside, and others have promoted further study and research. One finding that all research seems to validate is that children learn from role models as they observe. While there may be variation in some aspects of the findings, it is agreed that love, nurturing, and emotional connection to other people are crucial to healthy development.

The following poem by Dorothy Law Nolte (copyright 1972) expresses the power of learning through observation and experience (excerpted from the book *Children Learn What They Live*, 6–7; copyright 1998 by Dorothy Law Nolte and Rachel Harris; used by permission of Workman Publishing Co., Inc., New York; all rights reserved).

If children live with criticism, they learn to condemn.
If children live with hostility, they learn to fight.
If children live with fear, they learn to be apprehensive.
If children live with pity, they learn to feel sorry for themselves.
If children live with ridicule, they learn to feel shy.

If children live with jealousy, they learn to feel envy.

If children live with shame, they learn to feel guilty.

If children live with encouragement, they learn confidence.

If children live with tolerance, they learn patience.

If children live with praise, they learn appreciation.

If children live with acceptance, they learn to love.

If children live with approval, they learn to like themselves.

If children live with recognition, they learn it is good to have a goal.

If children live with sharing, they learn generosity.

If children live with honesty, they learn truthfulness.

If children live with fairness, they learn justice.

If children live with kindness and consideration, they learn respect.

If children live with security, they learn to have faith in themselves and in those about them.

If children live with friendliness, they learn the world is a nice place in which to live.

(Nolte 1972)

Kohlberg's Theory of Moral Development

As physical, emotional, social, and spiritual development occurs, language skills progress, and ethical development takes place in children. The family provides the foundation for the development of morals. Not only do we guide our children in decisions and provide care, nurturing, and a healthy environment, we guide their moral development as well. Lawrence Kohlberg, a professor at Harvard University for many years, developed three levels of moral reasoning, which he subdivided into six stages. Kohlberg, who began as a cognitive developmental psychologist, moved to the field of moral education, in which he spent years researching ethical and moral development.

Preschool and elementary school age children are in the first level, *preconventional.* At this level, people behave according to norms accepted by society because an authority figure advises them to do so. Obedience is seen in response to threats or punishment. This level has two stages, and as children pass to the second stage of level one, they learn that appropriate behavior means acting in their own best interest, in order to avoid negative consequences.

In the first stage of the second level, which is called *conventional,* a people behave in a way they believe will please others, especially authority figures. As they reach the second stage of the conventional level, they abide by laws and engage in socially acceptable behaviors while fulfilling duties and obligations.

Kohlberg and others believe that many adults do not reach the *postconventional,* or third, level. In the initial stage of this level, people show an understanding of social mutuality and interest in the welfare of others. In the final stage, people show, in their behavior, a respect for universal principles and respect for the individual conscience.

It is interesting to note that Kohlberg was inspired by the work of Piaget, although his stages do not parallel Piaget's stages. Both Kohlberg and Piaget, along with Erikson, realized that development occurs largely through social interaction as one passes from one stage to the next as a result of resolving conflict of specific areas of development. Unlike Erikson's stages of emotional-social development, which can be revisited and do not have to be fully completed, Kohlberg's theory professes that a person can only pass through one stage at a time, and a person does not move to the next without completion of the previous stage.

In closing our discussion of the theories of development, I would like to share Erikson's golden rule, "Do to another what will advance the other's growth even as it advances our own" (Erikson 1982, 93).

Chapter 2

*In*fancy: Getting to Know Each Other

Who has not responded with a softened heart when observing infants, especially when they are sleeping? They are so peaceful and innocent when asleep, so totally unaware of the huge impact they have on so many lives. They enter our world as dependent and sometimes demanding little people who capture our hearts and pull us into their worlds, casting their mystical spell over us, whether we are parents, family members, admiring friends, or caretakers. We want only the best for each infant, realizing that no infant asks to be born, and they are all in our care. It is our responsibility to nurture them and provide the care, love, and security to help them grow and develop. Our job as parents and caretakers includes providing unconditional love and nurturing, along with the more obvious necessities like shelter, food, and a safe haven.

This precious bundle can also create chaos and

frustration in our lives. Infants and young children are egocentric by nature, drawing us into their worlds as we adapt and try to meet their demands and needs without spoiling them. It is fascinating to see the dependent newborn develop into a mobile, verbal, and more autonomous individual with unique characteristics.

Both heredity and environment contribute to personality, and years of observation have shown that temperament remains consistent over time. Each infant is a unique individual, and as we get to know each one, we learn the best way to communicate and respond. We can expect that quiet infants will be quiet, introspective children and adults, who will internally process their observations. Hyperactive, easily stimulated infants will probably always be very active individuals who do best with routine times of quiet built into their day. It is truly amazing how children in one family, with the same parents, vary in personality, temperament, and responses.

Infant health, including physical and emotional, begins in the womb. Growing within a warm and cozy home, the fetus hears and senses what is going on in the environment. A pregnant mom, with the help of her family and support system, can provide a nurturing and healthy environment for the fetus by striving to be healthy both physically and emotionally, before and during pregnancy. If a pregnant mom has health concerns or is emotionally not at her best, it is important that she share her concerns with her physician and a spouse or partner, as well as those people in her immediate support system.

Postpartum depression, a state of depressed feelings

and sadness experienced by some birth mothers in the first few months after birth, is now receiving more attention, as it should. Postpartum depression has been recognized for decades but was not often talked about. Depression can vary from slight, with minimal or no impact on functioning, to severe symptoms, accompanied by feelings of hopelessness and worthlessness, which greatly impact the functioning of the mom and her ability to care for her infant. The mom's relationship with others is affected, in addition to the difficulty she may experience in bonding with her baby. Severe postpartum depression has been known in some cases to place the safety of the infant in danger. Fortunately, postpartum depression is openly acknowledged and talked about today. Health care providers have incorporated screenings for depression into their routine visits, and hospital maternity departments across the country take an active role in assessing moms for depression. If you are a new mom and experiencing sadness and depression, please consult your health care provider. If you are concerned that a family member or friend who has recently given birth is experiencing symptoms, encourage her to seek care. While many factors can contribute to postpartum depression, including hormonal changes, stress, anxiety, and worry, sleeplessness plays a part as well.

We continue to learn and understand more about the importance of mental health during pregnancy, infancy, and early childhood. The Infant Mental Health Organization, at state, local, national, and international levels, contributes to improving the emotional/mental and social health of infants and young children, beginning with the prenatal environment and continuing through early childhood. The Infant Mental Health Organization connects child health professionals who are devoted to promoting the well being of infants and young children. Through collaboration, the organization increases awareness of the importance of a healthy environment for infants and young children. Local groups address community needs and resources, as well as referral sources for assessment and interventions as needed. Some local groups have changed their name to include family wellness, but the mission remains the same.

As parents, we have difficulty cutting ourselves some slack as we strive to continue to keep up with demands. It is important that we realize the importance of caring for ourselves and letting go of less important things. Letting someone help with getting meals on the table, cleaning, and running errands is important while we focus on bonding with our infants and resting when the baby sleeps. Yes, we have all heard that many times, but sometimes it takes a while for some of us to realize it. I include myself in this slow-learning group because I was a work in progress as I tried to let things go. Sleep deprivation comes quite naturally with the newborn, as they require frequent feedings and their circadian rhythms may be different from ours.

Not only did lack of sleep affect my energy level, I was somewhat foggy brained, and a few times, maybe irrational. I look back on a couple of crazy things I did and think, *Was that me?* One incident that stands out is when my youngest daughter was only a few weeks old. Late one afternoon, which can be the witching hour, as everyone is tired from the day's activities, I noticed that my baby was sleeping through all kinds of commotion and noise, including her two older sisters yelling at each other. Not thinking clearly from sleep deprivation and fatigue, I immediately came to the conclusion that my baby had a hearing deficit. I placed her in her infant seat on the living room rug and rang a dinner bell to rouse her. She didn't wake up, but the ringing of the bell did quiet her sisters. As I sat on the living room floor crying, with a calm, sleeping baby and a dinner bell in front of me, my husband came home from work. Amid the chaos, he calmly asked what was wrong, and I told him I thought the baby was deaf because she slept through her sisters' noisy commotion and didn't respond to the dinner bell. He provided the voice of reason and logical thought as he reminded me that in utero the baby had periodically heard that type of interaction from her sisters, and she had become accustomed to the commotion of a busy home. He said not to worry, that she would wake up when she was ready. And guess what? She suddenly woke up. After that, I never worried about her hearing again, but I did feel foolish for overreacting. I was a pediatric nurse and an experienced mom; I should have realized the baby was used to sleeping through the normal noises of the busy household, but my foggy brain inhibited my logical thinking.

The infant's temperament influences individual behavior and reactions to the environment, just as our temperaments impact our interactions with our children. Sleep patterns vary among infants, which can pose challenges for parents. A baby's temperament, whether quiet, active, or in between, will influence reactions to the environment. Some babies seem more flexible, and others are less open to schedules. Over the decades, thoughts about schedules with infants have differed. Some experts advise keeping the baby on a strict schedule. In contrast, others suggest the parents be flexible and flow with the baby's needs and desires. I find both to be somewhat unrealistic. We cannot expect an infant to totally adapt to our schedules, no matter how structured or unstructured the schedules may be. Nor should parents completely adapt their lives to immediately meet an infant's demands. Somewhere in the middle, with patience and time, we can find a comfortable place. As parents and caregivers provide nurturing and love to meet the infant's needs, the infant learns to adapt, with encouragement, until a more comfortable routine is found, which meets the overall needs of the family. Consistency is helpful to all family members, although this may take some time and practice.

A quiet infant responds differently than an active or hyperactive infant. A quiet infant might wake for feedings quietly, with rarely a loud cry, and settle in easily for a nap after feedings, or quietly observe what is going on in the environment. An active or sensitive infant might have a more demanding cry and have difficulty falling asleep after feedings. Active or sensitive infants may flail their extremities around and fuss. They may respond to an overly stimulating environment with increased crying, or they may shut down. They may be more reactive to any increased noise and commotion in the home, thus requiring times of quiet and rest. The active infant may have more difficulties with transitions.

Infants observe their environment on their own terms

as their time awake increases. This alert time gives them an opportunity to become familiar with ways to amuse themselves and self soothe. Advice on responding to a baby's cry differs. One school of thought is to let babies cry so they don't learn to expect an immediate response every time they start to cry. Another recommendation is to respond immediately so they do not have unmet needs, adding to building frustration. Then, there is the middle-of-the-road advice, which I advocate and tried to practice. Yes, we need to meet the infant's needs, but an infant also needs to learn to self-soothe. Of course, any cry that indicates pain, illness, or fear needs to receive an immediate response so that we can find the cause.

Infants display different types of cries to express hunger, fatigue, pain, illness, and fear. Each infant has an individual way of expressing needs with crying. Some infants have a louder, more demanding cry to express hunger or frustration. Some infants may have a softer, whiny cry when sick. As parents get to know their infant, they are able to identify the type of cry more easily.

After checking for discomfort, illness, and hunger, a little fussing will not hurt. Babies do not need to be held whenever they are awake and they need an opportunity to learn to self-soothe. Some infants may settle down with holding, rocking, or quiet music. Sometimes touch and interaction help. Other times, infants may cease crying with a change of environment. Babies respond to their caregivers' emotions, and it is normal for parents and caregivers to feel anxiety when unable to comfort their infants. Taking a couple of deep breaths, or doing a couple stretches, before responding to the infant's crying may calm the adults' anxiety. I always found the best thing was to take several deep breaths to relax. Then after checking the baby for anything unusual, I would rock her and comfort her. Parents and caregivers can find information on safety, illness, crying, development, and other topics related to infants and children in the list of resources at the end of this book. One source I recommend is the guidebook written and published by the American Academy of Pediatrics.

My three daughters displayed different temperaments immediately after birth. As a newborn, my oldest daughter automatically awoke every three to four hours for feedings and was easily contented afterward. My second daughter, in contrast, was sensitive and active. She had her days and nights completely reversed for about six to eight weeks, and no matter what I did to keep her awake during the day, she would fall asleep. Around nine o'clock every evening, she awoke, raised her little head, and stared at the world with her big blue eyes, as if to say, "Okay, world. Here I am." Try as I might with encouraging wakefulness during the day and offering a quiet, non-stimulating environment at night to promote sleep, she functioned on her own time system. Around the age of six to eight weeks, one night she suddenly reversed her own schedule and slept twelve hours at night, from 7:00 p.m. to 7:00 a.m., which she continued to do. One thing I learned from this experience was that sometimes things happen in their own good time. While I believe it is important to try to guide children into a routine that works best for everyone, it is worthwhile to realize that compromise takes time and effort.

Although initially she did a quick switch from being awake often during the night to sleeping twelve straight hours through the night, my daughter had difficulty settling down when placed in her crib in the evening, after rocking and nursing. Today, it is recommended that infants sleep on their backs. In the 1970s, stomach or side sleeping was suggested. Either my husband or I would gently rub her back and pat her little bottom, which was soothing to her. If we stopped rubbing her back before she was asleep, she awoke and was restless. Through trial and error, we found a solution. After patting her bottom, I would place very light pressure on her bottom and then replace my hand with a lightweight stuffed animal. We also tried different music boxes to see which one was more effective. One evening, we ended up playing three music boxes, with separate soothing tunes, simultaneously. It was like magic! Instant relaxation and sleep by the time the music boxes wound down. This established yet another routine that worked well for all involved. For several weeks, after a few minutes, we would sneak in and remove the stuffed animal from the crib. She gradually learned to fall asleep with only the music boxes, without the slight pressure on her back. The lesson for us was that sometimes it takes several trials before finding an effective solution. This is true throughout life.

In the beginning, as we are getting to know our little one, everything is a new experience, and we may doubt our effectiveness. But with patience, we can find solutions. Every infant expresses individual needs in different ways, and we learn to find ways to meet both the needs of the infant and our own needs.

Around the time my second daughter was six months old, she had established her routine of sleeping twelve hours a night but seldom took long naps. In contrast to my other daughters, who were easily guided into two naps during the day—a short morning nap and a longer afternoon nap—my middle daughter was alive and energetic for a few hours after waking in the morning, and then she seemed ready for a nap about eleven in the morning. Any attempts on my part to stall her nap, or lengthen it once she fell asleep, didn't work. She seldom slept more than one and a half hours. Thus, by late afternoon, due to fatigue and overstimulation, her fussiness built to a crescendo, and she was difficult to console. It was the middle of winter, with early darkness, and for several days, I tried to comfort her with rocking, offering to nurse, or playing soft music. Nothing worked. She continued to cry inconsolably. One day, after trying different strategies, I placed her in her crib, alone in her room. I left a soft light on and played a music box with a soothing tune. She cried for a few minutes and then was able to soothe herself enough to fall asleep for fifteen to thirty minutes. When she awoke, she was better able to tolerate the evening routine, through feedings, bath, and a quiet bedtime. This became our daily routine for the next several months. With help, she learned to self-soothe, a tool that benefits us all, no matter our age.

Development is truly amazing and happens with such speed. Some babies seem to flow from one stage to the next, and touchpoints are less intense. Others may move from one stage to another quickly, leaving a parent to wonder what happened. For example, some babies gradually increase their sleeping at night and wakefulness during the day. Others may have an unpredictable wake-sleep schedule for what seems like forever, and then suddenly begin sleeping for longer stretches at night.

Dr. Brazelton (1992) identifies the following as approximate ages for touchpoints in the first year: newborn, three weeks, six to eight weeks, four months, seven months, nine months, and twelve months. He breaks the newborn *touchpoints* into two categories, the *newborn individual* and the *newborn parents*. Each baby has an individual temperament, and parents learn to respond to each child depending on temperament. Parents, with their individual temperaments, begin to find their path in communicating with their newborn, whether the baby is their firstborn or one of siblings. As discussed earlier, Dr. Brazelton advises that the entire family may be affected at touchpoint times.

After birth, newborns are suddenly breathing on their own which is a new experience. In the womb, they were warm and protected, and now they are becoming accustomed to the outside world. They may have felt crowded in the womb, and suddenly they have freedom to move around. While that freedom of movement may be liberating, it takes the infant time to adjust. Swaddling the infant is helpful to provide a sense of boundaries and comfort. Touch and cradling may be more comforting to some newborns than others. Bright lights are a new experience, and their vision is not focused as they begin to stare with wonder at the stimulation in their new environment.

The mouth is the first sense to develop in the newborn. During the first weeks, the newborn's jerky movements become smoother and more controlled. Growth spurts occur around three and six weeks, and infants become more alert after the first two to three weeks. Sometimes parents marvel at the changes that happen so quickly.

Lifting their heads is one of the first major accomplishments in motor development. After becoming accomplished at lifting their heads, they begin to turn the head from side to side, followed by lifting both the head and chest. They gain large motor control before moving on to fine motor development. Their grasps become more intentional by three to four months, although they do not gain the ability to transfer an object from hand to hand until around six to eight months. Around seven to nine months they are more adept at using their thumbs.

When infants are three to four months old they become more aware of their environment, and they are responsive and social. They are able to roll over, or rolling over is a work in progress. Around six to seven months, they begin to sit, progress to sitting alone without support, and then become mobile! Some babies may begin walking gradually, moving from crawling, to creeping, to standing while holding on to an object or a person's hand; they slowly and steadily venture to walk solo. Some babies may crawl in a different way, or seldom crawl, desiring to stand and walk. Then, suddenly they let go of a supporting object and take off walking. The baby's mobility affects everyone, as parents and caregivers baby proof the environment, providing safety for a curious, active infant who moves quickly from one spot to the next and seems to easily find things of interest. Maybe it is Mom's favorite book, Dad's favorite coffee cup, sitting near the edge of a table, or Grandma's glasses left on a coffee table.

Feeding themselves is another important step as infants manipulate food and become aware of different textures. Although it is time-consuming and messy for them to play with their food while attempting to feed themselves, this experience promotes fine motor skills.

Erik Erikson identified the first task of social and emotional development as establishing a sense of trust. During the first year of life, we lay a foundation for communication. If infants are nurtured and cared for, they learn to trust those who provide their care. Infants who do not receive emotional love and social exposure have difficulty establishing trust, due to unmet needs because of lack of nurturing. The behavior of others has shown them that they cannot count on someone to provide them with the care and enrichment they need for healthy development. Awareness on the part of the infants is not at a conscious level. Many of us have heard of the experiments in various orphanages where one group of infants received emotional and social care, in addition to having their physical needs met. The other group received only custodial care. Not surprisingly, the infants who received the emotional and social care developed emotionally and socially at the expected rate, while the infants receiving only custodial care had delayed emotional and social development. Some infants who did not receive social and emotional care stopped crying, as they learned caregivers did not respond.

Erikson believed the basic strength achieved from establishing a sense of trust is hope. If babies' needs are met, and they are nurtured and loved, they learn to trust and develop a sense of hope. Hope continues to be a strength that proves helpful across the life span. Erikson believed withdrawal, a concerning symptom, was prevalent in children who had not begun to establish a foundation of trust. Withdrawal can be displayed both emotionally and physically, and this lack of emotional engagement or physical activity with others can be a regular pattern in a child who is withdrawn.

Because Erikson's stages of social and emotional development are flexible, this does not necessarily mean that people who are nurtured as young children will never have their sense of trust tested. Throughout our lives, circumstances arise that may alter a strong sense of trust, but an individual who originally established a strong foundation can and will return to a sense of trust, although maybe with caution. Throughout life, we learn through experience that trust cannot be blind. Although a person may have a sense of trust and optimism in general, the individual learns that sincere trust in life and relationships is often earned.

Erikson professed that young children's emotional and social learning is primarily *sensorimotor*. This is congruent with Piaget's theory of children's cognitive development during the first eighteen to twenty-four months of life. Young children learn through seeing, touching, hearing, smelling, and moving. Through experience, they begin to learn what behavior is acceptable and what is not. Their sense of curiosity at times seems like an empty vessel, unable to be filled, as they continue to explore their environment physically, emotionally, and socially. They respond to others, including parents and caregivers.

We have all seen babies mimic others with facial expressions and movements, giving credence to the social learning theories that all children learn from observation, actions, and consequences at a young age. The works of Erikson, Piaget, and others contributed to the work of Dr. Burton White and his team at the Harvard Preschool Research Project in the mid to late twentieth century. Contemporary observations and findings also support these theories.

Dr. Alfred Adler believed the family environment is an infant's first social experience. This is the beginning of years of social interactions and communication. The child learns about love and caring from the family. Around three to four months, as the child becomes more social and responsive, family members begin to change their interactions with the baby. The child is now more fun; older siblings may find the child adorable and cute, or they may think the child is annoying as they struggle to adjust to the changes in everyone's schedules and the attention this tiny being captures. These interactions, as well as the interactions of other caregivers, continue to promote a sense of trust in infants as their needs are met.

Over the years, many ethicists, psychologists, theologians, and educators have determined that ethical development begins in the family of origin early in life. The foundation of ethics, or morals, is laid during infancy as children experience life in their small worlds. A strong sense of trust, the power of observation, and learning through the sensorimotor process, integrate to begin the formation of ethical development. The foundation of spiritual development is laid in infancy and early childhood through the family's beliefs and practice.

In their book *The 5 Languages of Love of Children* (2012), Dr. Gary Chapman and Dr. Ross Campbell discuss the five ways children interpret love and, as they get older, express their love as well as their need for love. The five ways are physical, verbal affirmation, quality time, gifts, and service. Infants and young children need all forms of love, but physical expression is the most important because they learn about the expression of love primarily through sensorimotor experiences. Infants receive love messages through caring physical touches and soft, loving voices. The physical touch is soothing to them. They thrive hearing words of gentle encouragement, and although they may not comprehend the meaning of the words, a gentle voice is soothing. Quality time is one of the best gifts we can give our children, beginning in infancy. All this is part of getting to know each child as an individual. Dr. Campbell and Dr. Chapman also remind us that parenting is an act of service.

There are many books advising parents and caregivers about safety, normal developmental stages, illness, injury, and communication. A list at the end of this book provides options for further reading. One book I strongly recommend is the guidebook written and published by the American Academy of Pediatrics.

Chapter 3

The Toddler: A Time of Wonder and Exploration

I have always been drawn to toddlers. Their energy feels contagious as they assert themselves and their sparkling eyes search the environment for new discoveries. Reaching twelve months, the beginning of toddlerhood, is a major milestone for all involved. Think of the development that has been accomplished in one short year! Tiny, dependent infants are now mobile individuals, asserting their preferences as they start the journey to independence. Curiosity pushes toddlers to explore, and through their exploring, they learn so much about the world.

Toddlers are unique individuals. Development in all areas moves rapidly in toddlerhood, the span covering twelve months of age to three years. In toddlers, we see personality traits strengthening, skills developing, and immeasurable energy as we try to keep up with them. Temperament determines toddlers' responses, and their play and interactions with others. Children with a quiet temperament will probably continue to have a quiet, introspective approach as they explore their environment, always observing. They may show less of an outward reaction to their discoveries, but they experience awareness. Toddlers who were active infants will most likely be physically active toddlers, and possibly more demanding. Sensitive children who were perceptive and easily stimulated as infants will continue to show these traits. Hyperactive children will be more easily distracted with a shorter attention span, often showing obvious delight in discoveries. Unhappy, tense children will engage in less play and will interact less with others in the environment.

Just as temperaments differ among children, development will vary among individual children, even within the same family. Some may walk before twelve months, others not until around fourteen months. At well-child visits, your pediatrician will assess your toddler's development. As we watch them grow, we cannot help but admire their stamina and uniqueness, even during the frustrating experiences when their wills clash with ours.

Sensorimotor provides the primary learning through sight, sound, touch, and smell as toddlers move around, interacting with their environment. As in infancy, toddlers use their mouths as an important sensory organ. Motor development is evident in toddlers as they walk, run, and climb with increasing ease and refine their fine motor skills through touch and manipulation of things in their environment. Feeding themselves is one form of sensorimotor learning for toddlers as they look at, touch, manipulate, smell, and examine the particles of food. Learning to use utensils encourages motor development, visual and spatial coordination, and it fosters a sense of independence. There is a strong interaction between motor development and emotional development during the toddler years.

Bright colors and textures, whether in food, toys, or other objects, are fascinating to toddlers. Stacking blocks, examining different toys and other objects and learning how they work, are of primary interest to toddlers, showing their motor and cognitive advances. Toddlers have a sense of object permanence, meaning that if a toy or other object is hidden, they will look for it. They begin to realize that the object still exists and did not completely disappear. They also have learned the concept of storage; when holding two objects in their hands, and a third object is offered, they will drop an object from one hand in order to accommodate the third object. As development progresses, they learn to work through and find a solution, perhaps placing one object in their mouth so they can grasp a third. Toddlers are beginning to learn about cause and effect.

We observe the social learning theory as we witness toddlers learning by observation and imitation. They imitate so many things they see older children and adults do. They may hold and interact with a doll or stuffed animal the way their parents hold and interact with them. They may imitate housekeeping and other chores, or they may imitate Dad or another adult with tools. If only we could bottle up a toddler's love of sweeping and cleaning, there might be more cooperation later on. As toddlers engage in symbolic play, mirroring people in their lives, they are processing what they have observed around them. Evidence of cognitive competence is shown through fantasy play as they show the ability to take in and conceptualize behavior and its meaning. They express their feelings, observations, and responses through play. With other children, they engage in parallel play, seldom looking at each other or making eye contact. A toddler may not acknowledge the other child, but we can see that toddlers have observed the behavior of their peers, as they demonstrate similar behaviors.

Toddlers can be picky eaters, and many parents worry that their toddler is not eating enough. Toddlers also have ideas that do not make sense to us, like not wanting different foods to touch on a plate, or preferring to eat a certain food a certain way. My middle daughter went through a phase between the ages of two and two and a half, eating a mustard, relish, and ketchup sandwich for lunch Monday through Friday. She would eat anything else I placed on her plate, as long as she had her sandwich. I took advantage of this and made sure I added protein, a vegetable, and fruit to her plate, along with her sandwich. She would eat it all, but if I offered her a ham and cheese sandwich, carrot sticks, and an apple, she would not eat. Interestingly, on weekends when her older sister and dad were home for lunch, she ate what everyone else ate. We never figured out the whys of her preferences, but after about six months, the phase ended. It worked well to ignore it and not struggle with her about her lunch. Over the years, research has shown that if you offer healthy toddlers nutritious foods, they will usually eat what their bodies need. It is not too early to introduce simple choices to a toddler, and simple choices around foods work well.

Toddlers can choose between two alternatives, but do not give more than two. Always keep the choices in your control. For example, if you offer a two-year-old two choices for lunch, make sure the choices are nutritious and available. Open-ended choices like "What do you want for lunch?" do not work well. If you want to stress protein, offer two protein choices, like meat or cheese. Always keep it in your control. At the same time, the toddler will feel important because you are offering a choice, which encourages independence. Simple choices help decision-making abilities to develop. Too many choices overwhelm young children.

Do not offer a choice about something you want to happen. For example, do not ask, "Do you want to go for a nap now?" Gently tell them it is time for a nap and follow the pre-nap routine. Routines and consistency are important so toddlers know what to expect. They may have difficulty with transitions from activity to activity, and they need guidance as they transition. A brief reminder before a transition is helpful. When it is time to get dressed, if a favorite green shirt is in the laundry waiting to be washed, take out two shirts and ask, "Do you want to wear the yellow shirt or the blue shirt?" This can help avoid frustration and tantrums.

Verbal interactions promote the toddler's speech. Language develops, beginning with babbling in infancy, followed by short words, and then the toddler progresses to short sentences. Toddlers often talk to themselves, and we may not have a clue as to what they are saying. We may grasp a word or two, but the rest is lost to us. To them, there is meaning in all that they say. In their monologues, they are recreating their world and telling us their thoughts and stories. Through play, they rework life as it is happening from their perspective. As we notice the tone of voice, the toddler's mood is evident, and we can often tell from the tone and facial expressions that they are imitating us or other important people in their lives.

Many times, toddlers are listening to us when we talk, even though they may appear to not be. There were times when I thought my toddler wasn't listening as I pointed to a picture or talked about a color; then suddenly she would surprise me with something like "Look at dark blue car" or "Where red block?" Toddlers are full of surprises.

Reading and the interaction that occurs between the toddler and reader encourage language development. Toddlers love to be read to and thrive on the interaction that takes place with the reader, as together they identify pictures in addition to reading. They like to hear the same story over and over, and they like the sound of rhyming. Toddlers love rhythmic games, especially if the games are set to music.

Stuttering is common in toddlers who are two or three-years-old. Their little minds are working faster than they are able to express themselves in words. They may become frustrated. The best way to respond is not to correct them but listen and encourage. Be patient, for they are frustrated enough with themselves.

Toddlers become more aware of personal space, and this space is precious to them as they slowly show their independence. This is a good time to introduce the concept of boundaries, such as knocking on a closed door or not infringing on the space of older siblings when they are involved in an activity. The introduction to boundaries can be done gently at an appropriate level the toddler will understand.

Toddlers begin to understand the concept of self and realize they are separate from other individuals and objects in their environment. They retain a self-centered perspective, as all young children do, as they try to assert independence through behavior and sometimes manipulation to get their own ways. This is part of normal development, as young children are normally egocentric, thinking that the world revolves around them and they are the center of the universe. As toddlers become more aware of the emotions of others, they begin to understand and demonstrate reciprocal love. They show this in many of their actions, such as hugging, smiling, bringing their beloved toy to someone to share, patting the arm or back of someone who may appear sad or ill, or behaving in ways to get the attention of a loved caregiver. Toddlers sense the mood of the environment and the emotions of others, without verbal interactions. Advances in social and emotional development are fascinating to watch in these little people.

Children learn when they are developmentally ready. We cannot force learning, but we can encourage it by providing appropriate stimulating and safe environments. Young children learn more through an emotional sense than cognitive; in other words, they remember feelings associated with actions rather than the facts. As they grow and show more independence, touch remains an important message of love to the toddler.

Dr. Brazelton identifies the touchpoint times in toddlerhood as twelve months, fifteen months, eighteen months, twenty-four months, and thirty-six months. Touchpoints may be more obvious in some children, like the active or sensitive child, than in other children. With each spurt of growth and development, children may regress slightly. They may be more intense in their reactions, or need more love and support when frustrated. They may experience a change in sleeping or eating patterns or be clingier with a primary caregiver. They may venture off into another room while playing or exploring but return frequently or call out to make sure a parent is still there.

Toddlerhood brings the first hint of noncompliance and negativism. Toddlerhood, especially the second year from two years to three years, has often been referred to as "the first adolescence." Toddlerhood is a transition from infancy to preschool, whereas adolescence is a transition from childhood to adulthood. In their book *The 5 Love Languages of Children* (2012), Dr. Chapman and Dr. Campbell advise not to confuse negativism with defiance. Negativism and defiance are two different things. Negativism is part of the normal stage of toddlerhood. Negativism is the child responding by saying no, either verbally or with actions. It is a toddler's way of pushing limits, and it may end in a tantrum. Defiance is open resistance to authority and is not acceptable.

Toddlers live with positive and negative emotions, just as adults do. Tantrums begin as a way for toddlers to express their feelings and independence. Tantrums represent an interaction between toddlers' motor and emotional development and reflect their inner struggle with the intensity and passion of their emotions. When children are feeling overwhelmed, hungry, or tired, tantrums may be more intense as they struggle even further for their independence. Just as adults need to express both positive and negative emotions, so do children. It is unhealthy to be passive and never express negative feelings.

Now is the time to begin teaching children appropriate ways to express negative feelings like frustration, sadness, and anger. Dr. Brazelton and others advise that opposite feelings may arise as toddlers try to express both negative and positive feelings. It is useless to try to talk to toddlers when they are in the middle of a tantrum. How many of us have left a store with a screaming child because the child's will contrasted with ours? We may feel embarrassed, or we may receive judging looks or looks of empathy from other parents. It is hard to remain calm when this happens, but it is important to remove the child from the situation and go to a quiet place. This gives the message that the behavior was unacceptable, although children may not learn that lesson immediately. They need reassurance and firm, consistent limits and boundaries, which provide security. Toddlers need to know you love them, but you do not like their behavior at the time. When they are upset, toddlers need support, not a contest of wills (Brazelton 1992).

Toddlers are beginning to learn about self-discipline now. They need guidance in finding ways to self-soothe, and often they will seek their favorite object for comfort. Toddlers will gravitate to their beloved object when feeling tired and overwhelmed. Many children give this special object its own name, such as "blankie" or "lovey." A word of advice: if your child has a favorite blanket or a love object (also referred to as a transitional object), early on, try to have your toddler adjust to two identical or similar blankets, so when one is dirty and needs to be laundered, there is another acceptable love object available.

It is our responsibility as parents and caregivers to structure the environment so toddlers are safe and can continue to develop. All toxic substances, including plants, medications, and dangerous objects must be placed out of their reach. A lot of the rearranging we do to accommodate the environment for toddlers will depend on the toddler. Some toddlers are fascinated with paper and will tear anything reachable, including books. Some toddlers are climbers and will scare adults at the rate they climb to tops of bureaus or backs of furniture. Now is also a time when toddlers begin to learn the meaning of the word *no*.

Structuring the environment for safety lessens frustration for the toddler. Think of this environmental control as a way to provide a safe environment for curious toddlers, while stimulating their curiosity as they explore and learn. The more a parent or caregiver has to say no, or limit a toddler's exploration, the more frustrated both the toddler and caregiver become. So, set limits and be consistent. This way, children are aware of their boundaries and what will happen next. One-step, short requests are more effective at curbing the toddler's frustration. Pick your battles.

Discipline is about *teaching* and *guiding*, which is what we do as parents and caregivers when we show children the best way to do things and appropriate ways of behavior. Discipline is not punishment, but a means of guidance. Discipline should be done with love. Pick your battles and maintain consistency. Dr. Fitzhugh Dodson, a child psychologist who authored several books on development and discipline in the 1970s and 1980s, suggested that rapport is the emotional foundation of all discipline. He stressed the importance of a positive, healthy relationship between the child and parent. If the love and bonding that began in infancy continues discipline is more effective.

When my children were toddlers, we left a few important unbreakable items around, and each child began to learn the meaning of respect for other people's things. Each of my daughters was different in her approach. My oldest daughter loved books and would pull books off the lower bookshelves. She would sit on the floor and stare at the pages of the book, and if one didn't know better, one might think she was actually reading the way her eyes moved across the pages as she turned them. She never attempted to tear pages of a book, but she liked to tear paper book covers. Thus, we removed all paper book covers from books at her level. Sometimes she would stack one book on top of another, like she did with her blocks. My middle daughter tore any paper in sight, even tissues, so tissues and toilet paper were not within her reach. And my youngest daughter showed more interest in her older sisters' toys than in tearing paper. My middle daughter was a climber who would fearlessly climb anything, so one of our focuses was keeping her safe. We removed any chair she could move and use to climb to a higher object from rooms where she played, and in her room. We structured the environment a little differently for each one, depending on each one's needs and fascinations, as well as safety concerns.

Autonomy, a healthy sense of self, is the second developmental task according to Erik Erikson's theory of social and emotional development. Walking alone is the first biggest step toward individuation. We see toddlers' autonomy, or independence, as they assert themselves and learn to do things more independently. It is important to remember that no one achieves total independence. Interdependence is the goal of healthy development, as a person learns self-care, while being able to function in society and maintain successful relationships. Autonomy is the will of one's actions and thoughts, and each child who individuates achieves a sense of will. Children who successfully pass through this stage will have the foundation of the strength of will. They have learned to trust and therefore have hope. Now they have the will and desire to accomplish.

If children do not pass through this second stage, they are at risk for feeling shame and may have doubts about their abilities in the future. They may not have the will or desire to accomplish tasks as individuals that they might have attempted with less doubt and a stronger will.

Erikson believed that if children do not develop the trait of will they may have compulsive traits. They may show compulsiveness with punctuality or a need for orderliness and organization. Compulsive traits may also surface with traits of thriftiness or restricted affections. This is not to be confused with the diagnosis of OCD (Obsessive Compulsive

Disorder), which presents symptoms that can impact a person's functioning. Often, we hear comments like "She's OCD," or, "He is so obsessive about ..." It is important to remember that we might have obsessive or compulsive traits pertaining to one area, but that does not mean we have OCD. Some people have compulsive traits about doing a task a certain way, like folding towels a certain way or following a certain process for washing dishes. If this does not interfere with daily functioning, it should not be a problem. Most people are aware if they tend to have obsessive thoughts or perform actions in a compulsive and rigid way.

The foundation for the development of ethics and spirituality continues to expand. Conscience is not innate or inborn; it is learned. Toddlers begin to internalize values they see modeled by family and other people who are important in their lives.

Roles within the family and family interactions continue to provide toddlers with a foundation for communication and socialization. Dr. Adler and his associates pointed this out years ago, as did Erikson. In his book *The First Three Years of Life* (1975), Dr. Burton White, of the Harvard Preschool Project, stated, "The informal education that families provide for their children makes more of an impact on a child's total educational development than the formal educational system" (White 1975, 4). Sibling interaction contributes to the toddler's ways of interacting with others. A toddler with a sibling only one to two years older may learn to be defensive in some situations if the interactions with an older sibling promote this type of response. A toddler with a sibling three or more years older may have a more affectionate relationship with the older sibling, or may thrive in the attention received from the older sibling. Often, with three or more years between siblings, the youngest may be left alone as the older ones gravitate toward their own activities. As parents and caregivers, we can promote a positive environment to encourage the development of each child and strengthen the family unit.

Spending quality time with toddlers is important to their development. Often, short and maybe more frequent intervals work best for quality time. For example, it is helpful if young children know that before nap or bedtime, they have special reading time. A routine gives toddlers time to shift their thought process and realize what is happening next.

The "terrible twos" is a cliché often used to describe toddlers. I find toddlers to be delightful, engaging little people who are beginning to exert their independence as they explore everything in their environment and move into autonomy. They take pride in accomplishing new things as they move to the preschool ages.

Chapter 4

The Preschool Child: The Power of Play and Pretend

Childhood is a time filled with adventure, excitement, and learning. The preschool years, between the ages of three and six years, are powerful. Children acquire knowledge and abilities rapidly as they learn through play, games, creativity, communication, observation, reading, and other activities. Play is a very important part of development for preschool children. The majority of learning and brain growth occur in the first five to six years of life. Following Erikson's theory of social and emotional development, preschool children learn and problem-solve through play. They begin to understand more about themselves and their world. As parents and caregivers, we can enhance preschool children's learning experience by providing them with an environment that enhances their learning, creativity, strengths, socialization skills, and identity.

Young children enjoy learning. In addition to learning

through play and imitation, they learn by helping with simple chores and taking age-appropriate responsibility. Preschool children express their feelings through play. Play encourages a positive self-concept and helps form a sense of self. Play also helps them relate to others, leading to gains in social and communication skills. Play promotes language development, stimulates thinking, and lays the foundation for beginning problem solving. Play enhances creativity as the imagination offers different ways of thinking. We witness the remarkable gains in neurological and motor development when they go from walking to running to skipping. Their increasing agility in large and fine motor skills and coordination is amazing.

While we witness their growth, it is important to remember that individuals develop at different rates and that development varies. Some children may have more advanced verbal and language skills; others may display strong motor skills. The range of normalcy varies. No one develops according to a perfect scale, and norms should be used as guidelines. Everyone has weaknesses or areas of lesser strength, and parents and caregivers can help children find ways to strengthen weaknesses if an area seems to be developing more slowly than others. For example, if a child is slow at climbing, help by offering simple, safe activities that will strengthen limitations. If your child is very shy, you can help by gradually exposing the child to small, quiet groups to increase comfort with other people.

If a preschool child is having difficulty with fine motor development, parents and caregivers can offer opportunities for the child to strengthen fine motor skills. It is healthy for preschool children to realize that no one is perfect and that no one does everything easily. Different people have different strengths, and everyone has areas that they are not proficient in. Children learn that help is available to strengthen areas that are not as strong, and some things may take more effort. This is also part of learning respect for others and their differences. If you have concerns about any area of your child's development, it is wise to consult your health care professional.

Children seem to intuitively sense their strengths and weaknesses and may use the excuse "I don't like to do that" to mask an area they sense to be inferior. You can help children build their strengths by encouraging them to use their talents. Some children are, by nature, more athletic; others may show promising music or artistic abilities, and others may be more gregarious in their interactions with peers. Awareness of the child's temperament and individual responses is important as we offer opportunities for growth and development. Perhaps children's strengths were beginning to show their presence in the toddler years, but now they are more obvious. Through play, we can help preschool children nurture their strengths and improve weak areas.

All young children have creative abilities, and these abilities need to be nurtured in a healthy and safe way. There are many ways preschool children can use their special gift, whether it is in arts and crafts, social communication, dramatic play, or physical activities. During their creative play, children may imitate and mirror the behaviors and emotions of others, whether these are witnessed in person or through television or other technology. Creativity offers important information to adults about children's thoughts, preferences, and even problems they may be trying to solve and work through.

Drama is a major part of the preschool child's play experiences. As parents and caregivers, we can monitor the dramatic play to be sure it is healthy and not influenced negatively by social media and other forms of technology. Television and other electronics should be limited and monitored. It is tempting to have children watch a television show, watch movies, or play educational games on their Leapfrogs or other learning devices. During that time, we as parents and caregivers can accomplish tasks or have some much-needed quiet time. When possible, watch movies and appropriate television shows with your children and discuss what you watch, pointing out reality versus fiction. Briefly talk about the feelings of the characters and how they may be affected by the story. This will encourage the child to understand emotions of others and how events impact our emotional lives. Not only does this activity of sharing promote social interaction and communication with the exchange of thoughts, these discussions can be good learning experiences for all involved. To make this a learning experience, we need to remember preschool children have a short attention span, think concretely, and relate best to simple ideas.

Play for preschool children includes pretend, imitation, and imagination, while they observe the behavior and attitude of adults, teens, older children, and peers. How many little boys have been Superman or Captain America, and how many little girls have been fairies or princesses?

Through pretend play preschool children try out different roles and various ways to express themselves. Preschoolers are developing the ability to compare and contrast what they observe in their environment. This is all part of their world as they incorporate fantasy and real life.

Having an imaginary friend, or even more than one, is common for the preschool child. Sometimes an imaginary friend is a source of reassurance and companionship, and a child seeks this imaginary friend when in need of reassurance, love, or security. Imaginary friends may take on positive qualities preschool children admire in others and wish for themselves. This is an example of wishful thinking, which is part of the preschooler's daily life. Sometimes the imaginary friend is a playmate, and the child actively involves the imaginary friend in many activities. At these times, preschool children believe their friend is present, and they believe you experience the imaginary friend too. Sometimes an imaginary friend is the scapegoat, and the child can transfer the feeling of "badness" to the imaginary playmate. Many times, the imaginary playmate receives the blame for negative behavior and things that happen, like spilled milk, the disappearance of an object we might be looking for, or the reason the child hit a sibling. This is not done out of spite or to avoid the truth; it does not happen because the child is being mean. It is because children sometimes have difficulty distinguishing reality from wishful thinking, and they need gentle guidance. Sometimes this wishful thinking places them in a position of feeling responsible for something negative that happened.

Children need help to understand it wasn't their thinking that caused an event.

Children in this phase of development may say they hear voices telling them to do something. They are not psychotic or having auditory hallucinations. The voices they state they hear are a product of their imaginations as they figure things out and try to understand life. Preschool children, and sometimes, older children, will say they did something wrong because somebody, maybe an imaginary friend, told them to do that. Some children will cleverly say their brain told them to do something. This is because of the struggle going on within their consciences. To relate to Erikson, Freud, and other theorists, there is an internal struggle between the id (basic drives) and the superego (conscience). The basic drive, the id, tells a child to take money from his mother's purse, and the conscience, or superego, argues with the id, saying, "No, it is wrong. You will be punished. You should not do it." The id returns with, "Do it. Don't get caught. Let someone else be blamed and punished." This internal struggle feels confusing, and children may not know how to resolve the problem. The quickest way may be to assign the blame to someone, or something else.

Preschool children do not intentionally lie to be mean or vindictive. Referring to Kohlberg's theory of moral development, preschool children are at the preconventional level of moral development, where they realize if they do something wrong, they will be punished. They want to avoid punishment, so they blame someone or something else, even an imaginary person or object. Or they may say their brain told them to do it. They may think that not being truthful protects their wish to avoid confrontation. They also have difficulty distinguishing reality from fiction and need help in understanding the difference. As their conscience starts to work, they will experience guilt, and because they don't know how to process it, or may not even understand it, they may react with anger.

This is a teaching opportunity for the adult, whether parent or caregiver, to explain the importance of truth, trust, and respect, as well as the effects untruths can have on others. Of course, this needs to be explained at a level the child can understand and in a way that encourages the child to realize consequences. It is important to do it in a way that doesn't undermine the child's self-esteem.

Through development and time, children progress to awareness of needs and thoughts and feelings of others. The preconventional stage of morality may extend to elementary school-age children, and even to some adolescents. Kohlberg and others have identified intelligent adults who function at this level of moral thinking. Such people make decisions based on what is best for self, without regard for others. They obey rules established by powerful authority figures to avoid punishment, and they may disobey if they are not likely to be caught.

Research by many developmental specialists shows that morals begin rather naturally in a loving parent-child relationship, and conscience is learned as morals become internalized through guidance and learning. Around the age of four, children begin to show more internalization of values. Environment, including the actions of others that the child observes and experiences, play a part in the formation of morals and ethics.

Young children today are exposed to so many parts of life that are frightening and too mature for them to handle. They may respond by mimicking what they heard through the media or a conversation. Children in anger may make a comment that seems concerning. They may feel sad, angry, or frightened, but in reality, they do not want to hurt anyone. They are desperate and want to be removed from the situation but don't know what to do, so they repeat what they have heard. Children at this age do not understand the consequences of their statements or the finality of death. This is the time for a reality check, and an adult can help children understand the seriousness of what they are saying. If a child is presenting as sad and hopeless, negative or aggressive, it may be time for an assessment by a professional.

Many preschoolers are attached to a favorite blanket, and this transitional object provides security. The object is also a source of love and comfort, and it is important that we acknowledge this significance. Boundaries can be set for the places the love object can accompany children. For example, it should be available for bedtime and in the home any time a child needs it. Sometimes it is helpful for the object to accompany the child in the car. If the object accompanies the child in the car, I find it best to suggest the object remain in the car while errands are done or the child is in preschool. This way, the object does not get dragged from store to store, and there is less chance of losing it. However, some daycares and preschools encourage children to have a transitional object with them. In this case, think about having two, one for home and one for daycare/preschool. Laundering the blanket can be a problem, as the child may not want to part with it. In this case, I find it works best to explain that, just like the child needs a bath, so does the blanket (or other object), and after washing, the blanket will be all soft and cuddly. Children can be weaned from their beloved item as they are ready. For example, start by eliminating the times the transitional object accompanies them in the car. Gradually, the object will be used only at bedtime. This adjustment takes time, but often as language skills increase, they need the object less.

Imaginary friends are a huge part of the preschool child's life, and they enter our lives as well. We may set a place at the dinner table for the imaginary friend, or we may be expected to give the imaginary friend, or favorite stuffed animal or doll, a good night hug and kiss. It is not unhealthy to allow the child to indulge in this fantasy world, as long as we guide them in their awareness of reality versus fiction. The imaginary friend's age, living place, and status may change over time.

My oldest daughter had an imaginary friend when she was four. This friend lived with us for several months. The imaginary friend began as a four-year-old who moved in to play with my daughter, who at the time had no siblings. Sometimes the friend shared meals with us, traveled in the car with us, or reportedly slept next to my daughter's bed. Other times, the friend was mysteriously absent, and the reason provided was that she was visiting her other family. After a few months, the imaginary friend suddenly aged.

She was a seventeen-year-old, and she was the big sister. At the time, I was pregnant with my second daughter, and about a week before my second daughter was born, my oldest daughter announced to us that her friend grew up, got married, was having a baby and moving to New York. When asked why the friend moved to New York, my four-year-old responded that her friend wanted to be in the big city near Sesame Street. We accepted her explanation and half-expected the imaginary friend to return in some form, but she never did.

I have heard of and have been introduced to many imaginary friends over the years by many children I have been associated with. Family members have told me that I had imaginary friends as a child. I remember quite a bit of my preschool years, but I do not remember my imaginary friends. My experiences with imaginary friends were sometimes the topic of family entertainment over the years. Apparently I had a pseudo-identity because around the time I was four and a half, when I was playing, I was Mrs. Jones. Mrs. Jones had a husband, Mr. Jones, and a friend I named Mrs. Woodrin. My mom always said I did not know anyone by that name, and that I had made it up. My dolls were my children. I was told several times about one humorous incident that occurred when I was five. About eight or nine months after my dad passed away, my mom, my aunt, and I were driving to Maryland to visit my uncle, aunt, and two cousins. I have been told that I insisted my husband and Mrs. Woodrin accompany us. Apparently, my mom said they could ride partway with us, but we would have to leave them off somewhere to visit because there would not be room at my uncle's house for everyone. My mom said she told me I could let them know when and where we were to leave them off. According to the story, driving through Massachusetts, I suddenly yelled, "Stop! They are going there to visit." My mom and aunt laughed about that for years, because the place I designated was an uninhabited old shack at the entrance to woods. From what I have been told, my "friends" stayed there, because we never picked them up on the way home, and they never surfaced again. As I reflect on this childhood experience, I wonder if I created this imaginary family and friend because, as a four-year-old, I was observing the disintegration of my nuclear family as my father became more ill. After he passed, maybe it was important to me to establish the security of a family, even if it was temporary and imaginary, so I gave myself another name when I played. I had an imaginary husband, and Mrs. Woodrin was my trusted friend. Somehow, during the trip to Maryland, I must have unconsciously felt that I no longer needed the security of my imaginary family and friend. I am only guessing about the reason for my invention of these two imaginary people in my life at that time, but given the dynamics and all that was occurring, these friends fulfilled a need for me at that time. I think this is often the case; an imaginary friend provides security, companionship, someone to play with, or someone to blame.

Preschool children love to be read to. Reading is a quiet activity that you and your child can do together, and it can continue to be a shared activity as the child learns to read. Reading promotes the development of cognitive, language, and interaction skills, as well as development of the imagination. It stimulates the child's mind and opens the child to other possibilities. Encourage your child to think about different possible endings for stories and talk about the characters in the story and the meaning of the story. Encourage your child to draw a version of a character or something that happened in the story. These activities will expand reading to a rich experience of communication and imagination. When selecting literature for the preschool child, consider recognizable people, animals, and objects with one main character. Stories with simple lines, action, and adventure are best. Rhymes fascinate the mind of preschool children, and with their expanding language skills, they love rhyming. Clear and colorful pictures promote visual stimulation and help children understand a story. Preschool children will listen to the same story over and over again and never tire of it. Soon, they have memorized much of the story and begin to say they are reading as they recite from memory. This is all part of learning and expressing themselves.

Communicating with grandparents or other family members is fun for children. They are not able to write letters yet, but they can talk about their experiences on the telephone or Face Time. Face Time is great, but having preschool children draw pictures to tell family members about their life is meaningful communication as well.

Children experience pleasure playing with simple things like cardboard boxes, kitchen utensils, and blocks. While many of the current toys offer wonderful learning opportunities, children use their imagination and creativity to fashion a tent over a kitchen table, or imitate an adult cooking. They play games like house, restaurant, and school. And, yes, even doctor. Playing doctor is curiosity about the body and reenacts a preschool child's experiences with medical care.

Like toddlers, preschool children delight in games and rhyming. Games are fun, and they contribute to development in many ways. Preschool children often like to make up their own versions of games. Simple board games offer a cognitive experience as well as sharing, interacting, and improvement in fine motor coordination. Games with categories are popular with preschool children as they learn about groups, categories, and matches. Puzzles help with hand-eye coordination. Games with geometric shapes foster imagination and creativity. Building blocks and Legos are useful in helping children increase motor skills and coordination as they construct their own creations.

Arts and crafts, including coloring, drawing, clay, painting, and finger painting, are fun, promote fine motor coordination skills, and are a wonderful way for self-expression. I am a fan of journaling for self-expression. Preschool children can journal with drawing. I have found that drawing and talking about fears, anxieties, and dreams encourages children to express themselves. Nature walks and age-appropriate athletics, along with general physical activities like running, jumping, and climbing, provide learning and social skills. Music is fascinating to preschool children, and it often provides rhyming, words, and physical activity.

Preschool children love to help plan and prepare meals with an adult, and this gives them an opportunity to enhance coordination as well as social and cognitive skills. They take great pride when family members enjoy and praise their efforts, and helping to plan meals gives them the chance to begin comprehending planning and organizing skills at their level. Children become aware of gender differences during this time. A little girl may imitate her mom, and a little boy may imitate his dad. This is the time when a little girl worships her dad and a little boy idolizes his mom.

As children's vocabulary expands, their curiosity shows with all the questions they ask. Endless questions hallmark the preschool child's life. "Why?" "How come?" Their curiosity is bubbling over, and they want to understand more about the world they live in. It is important to respond to their questions in a way that promotes understanding. Some children wonder about the people on television. "How did they get there?" "Who invited them to our house and why don't they come out of the television?" "Why are the people talking to me, but they won't answer me when I talk to them?" Questions like these are common. Once the child understands the television is projecting images like a camera, they begin to understand. All children ask where babies come from. When his parents told my grandson at the age of three that they would have a new baby at their house after Christmas, he asked, "Where is the baby now?" His parents responded the baby was growing in a special place inside Mommy, near her belly. Then he asked, "Mommy, why did you eat the baby?" Priceless. With his logic at that time, the belly was for food, which you ate. Therefore, his statement was logical for his stage of development. Questions and statements like this open the door for more teaching.

Children's statements give us an idea of what and how much they understand. There is a saying: four-year-olds ask all the questions, and seventeen-year-olds have all the answers. So if you feel impatient with the continuous questions, even the silly ones, remember that when your child is seventeen, all the answers will be provided!

Language skills continuously increase throughout childhood. Parents and caregivers can use any time they are together to incorporate communication—while cooking dinner, folding laundry, riding in the car together, or walking. Children respond to this; they feel important and love conversation. As language skills improve, preschoolers realize the power of words. This is something parents and caregivers can take advantage of, by encouraging children to use their words. Children need to learn to express feelings in a healthy way. They need to understand that it is healthy to express feelings.

Like toddlers, preschool children may disintegrate after daycare/preschool. Sleep is important to preschool children. Some children experience difficulty with sleep, either falling asleep or waking in the middle of the night. Preschool children need to learn to fall asleep on their own and feel secure. Bedtime is smoother if the same routine is followed nightly. The routine should be a quiet, relaxing time, not one filled with physical activity or emotional matters. A bath can be relaxing, followed by brushing teeth and a bedtime story. Many children love to have more than one story, and this works if time allows. Some children do better with a nightlight on. A monster check may be part of the routine for some. Children find it comforting to have their favorite love object, blanket, or stuffed animal at bedtime. Some parents find rubbing the child's back at bedtime is soothing. Some children like to have a favorite song sung. Whatever works for both the child and parent as a nightly routine is comforting to the child.

Preschool children, like toddlers who are beginning to talk, often stutter and it is usually because their minds are working faster than their speech. Do not supply the words or become exasperated. Give them time and space to express themselves. If they need help, they will ask. If they become frustrated, help them by asking how you can help.

Communication is both verbal and nonverbal. Nonverbal messages make up a large portion of communication that occurs in our daily lives. Tone of voice, facial gestures, stance, and body movement all relay important messages. Positioning our bodies a certain way, like crossing the arms in front of the body, can indicate that we are not interested, or we are defensive, or impatient. Pointing a finger while talking can be interpreted as threatening, even if our intentions are well meaning for the purpose of getting a point across. Tone of voice should match the words spoken. Verbal and nonverbal communication should be congruent, meaning they give the same message. A busy caregiver or parent can say in an offhanded way, in a monotone voice, with arms crossed, "Come here so I can give you a hug." The child may pick up on the nonverbal message and feel confused. Open arms, with some interest in the voice gives a more welcoming message.

With each progression in development come the touchpoint times. Dr. Brazelton (1992) identifies the touchpoints in the preschool stage as two, three, four, five, and six. At three, children may be more aggressive, and then settle into being quieter and more introspective. Around three and a half years of age, they begin to understand time and space. For example, they understand that after outside play at daycare and circle time, their parents will pick them up. Around three years of age, they begin to realize words can make things happen. At four, with their increased language skills, they begin to see the rewards of growing up and are motivated to learn new skills. As they approach five, preschool children become more aware of the feelings of others and how others might be affected.

Temperament remains consistent. Preschool children who were quiet, introspective infants and toddlers will maintain the same traits, often evidenced in their responses. Active, assertive children will probably engage in more physical activities and may be more easily distracted, showing a shorter attention span. Some children display more energetic responses, needing firmer limits and structure. The approach to sensitive children may involve more gentle guidance. Shy or sensitive children may need a different type of guidance and encouragement. Understanding our children's temperament is a guiding force in parenting. Different types of parenting and responses may have different effects, depending on a child's temperament. No matter what the characteristics of temperament are, preschool children are normally egocentric, feeling they are the center of the universe. With time and developmental progression, this will change, as they are able to develop greater empathy and understanding of the reactions of others. This often occurs around the age of five.

Along with the primary needs of sleep, hunger satisfaction, and other bodily needs, Dr. Brazelton identifies three characteristics that vary with each child's temperament and influence how an individual deals with the world. The first characteristic is task orientation, such as attention span, persistence, the degree of distractibility, and the activity level. The second is the child's social flexibility; for example, is the child's approach one of observation, exuberant interest, or withdrawal? How does the child handle and adapt to stimuli from the environment? The third assesses the child's reactivity. What is the child's responsiveness like? What is the intensity of the reactions, and what is the quality of the child's mood? All these enter into how a child responds to the environment, and it may vary if the child is tired or having an off day.

A mother's pregnancy is a touchpoint. Another touchpoint happens when the new sibling arrives and the family readjusts. As a preschool child's new sibling begins to crawl and get into the child's toys, yet another touchpoint may occur. As the younger sibling develops, the preschool child may show some regression and be more demanding (Brazelton 1992).

It is not uncommon for preschool children to alternate between shyness and exuberance. They may experience times of being more inward focused and other times they may be more outgoing. They may regress with fatigue or stress. They may experience anxiety or fear with unfamiliar objects or people. Around the age of four, behavior may be more exuberant, sometimes referred to as the "out-of-bounds fours."

Tantrums can still occur when children are frustrated, tired, or overwhelmed by stimulation in the environment. Children are often frightened by their own anger and their reactions. Language skills have improved, and this is an important time to help preschool children learn to use words and other acceptable ways to express frustration and anger. As their vocabulary expands, preschool children begin to use words rather than aggression to solve problems. A structured environment will help preschool children avoid tantrums before they escalate, by decreasing stimulation and helping children recompose. This takes time and practice as we observe our children's individual tolerance level and ways of handling stress and stimulation.

Fears may surface during the preschool period. Children around the age of five to six may have increased fears, such as fearing their family will not return home. Dr. Brazelton refers to the common fears as "ghosts from the nursery" (Brazelton 1984, 37). A child may become afraid of the dark or worry about monsters. This is part of their development, so go along with the child's questions, such as, "Can a monster get in while I'm sleeping?" Even though these thoughts and fears are in part due to their imagination, the fears are very real to children, and they need reassurance. A quick parental check under the bed or in the closet to assure them no monsters are present is worth the effort.

Learning to accept age-appropriate responsibility is part of the journey to adulthood and interdependence. Children need guidance and role modeling to learn and practice age-appropriate responsibility. It is important to have preschool children be accountable for simple chores. Preschool children can help by taking their dishes to the kitchen after a meal or snack, putting their dirty clothes in the hamper or another designated place, or picking up their toys. Picking up an entire room will be overwhelming, so encourage them to pick up small areas and offer to help. An effective strategy is "If you pick up the blue pieces, I will pick up the yellow." Chat with them while you do it together. Encourage them to pick up coloring toys when they finish coloring and before they move on to another activity. These strategies may not work all the time, but they are a step in the right direction. Children are receiving the message that they have some responsibility for themselves. Part of this responsibility is learning about respect—for self, others, and property. Children will feel proud of themselves and their accomplishments as they realize they are growing up. They are also learning that part of parenting is not picking up everything for everyone all the time.

Making choices is another area of responsibility. You will play an important role in helping your children make decisions, and they will look to you for guidance and encouragement. If children learn the basics of decision-making skills at an early age, they will have a foundation to build on as they grow. Like toddlers, preschool children are capable of only simple choices with two, and no more than three, simple options. Open-ended choices are not always appropriate, especially when choices contradict limits already set by adults in charge. Options should remain within the adult's control.

Through play, preschool children learn about their world. They begin to understand the difference between reality and fiction. According to Erikson's social and developmental theory, preschool children have gained trust, through which they gain the virtue of hope. Through autonomy, they develop the strength of will. The developmental task of the preschool years, referred to by Erikson as the "play years," is establishing *initiative* versus *guilt*. By establishing initiative, children develop the *strength of purpose*, and they begin to realize there is a purpose to what we do. Erikson believed the negative aspect, occurring when a person does not reach a successful level of attainment of initiative, is *inhibition*. Children who have not learned to feel comfortable with initiating may feel inhibited, which might prevent them from attempting tasks they are capable of accomplishing. Through all this, it is important to remember the child's individual temperament. Quiet and introspective children, shy children, and sensitive children may show different responses than assertive, active, or easily distracted children, and as parents and caretakers, we may find that our effective responses vary, depending on the child's temperament.

Piaget identified the preschooler as being in the *preoperational* stage of cognitive development, occurring approximately between the ages of two and seven years of age (Schell and Hall 1997). This stage begins with language acquisition and overlaps with social and emotional development. Piaget recognized it as the time when children are adept at manipulating symbols and they engage in symbolic play. For example, they readily use a broom for a horse or a small cardboard box for a frying pan. Preschool children are very concrete and will continue to develop a more logical, concrete approach in the years to come. We need to keep in mind that because preschoolers are egocentric, they have difficulty understanding the points of view of others.

Preschool children need ongoing cuddling, love, and quality time. Touch remains an important part of the message of love. Children need to feel valued and validated. Validation of strengths and positive behavior doesn't mean you are condoning negative behavior. You are valuing and loving the whole person, guiding the individual to make appropriate decisions and engage in appropriate behavior. In their book *No Drama Discipline: The Whole Brained Way to Calm the Chaos and Nurture Your Child's Developing Mind* (2011), Daniel Siegel, MD, and Tina Payne Bryson, PhD, discuss reconnecting with your child after miscommunication. First, connect. Then, redirect, remembering, "What lesson do I want to teach my child?"

All children need a nurturing environment that encourages them to build their strengths and develop to potential. Preschool children have tremendous potential, and it is our job to nurture that. The nurturing environment that gives unconditional love and support, stimulates curiosity, encourages age-appropriate exploration, and provides guidance, is a bonus for preschool children. A structured environment includes routines and promotes the most positive experience for preschool children, as it does for toddlers. Structure, routines, and boundaries offer children security, and they know what will come next. Routines also help the child to understand time. Through observation, imitation, and learning, both in their environment and from the people they have bonded with, preschool children are active participants in their journeys to adulthood and interdependence.

Mealtime can be an important ritual during which family members enjoy communication. To promote a positive experience, focusing on the communication and not the child's picky eating preferences is helpful. It is often difficult for families to have meals together because of busy schedules, but this is one time that family members can come together for a short time to communicate. As my children got older and involvement in activities limited the times we could eat dinner together, we began eating breakfast together as a family on school mornings. To be honest, sometimes the communication occurred only between my husband and me. My daughters were convinced we were the only family on the planet strange enough to eat breakfast together. But we persisted, and I am glad we did. To this day, as adults, my daughters remember breakfasts together.

Part of the structured environment includes remembering that preschool children will still experience difficulty with transitions and change. They need to be prepared for these times and not be surprised. Transitional objects, like a lovey, a blanket, or favorite stuffed animal, are important to children. It is important for children to know when their parents are leaving, and for them to have an idea of when their parents will return. Some children like to keep an object of the parent's, or a picture, so they feel close to the parent.

Discipline, which is teaching and guiding, is part of

the structured environment designed to keep children safe and meet their needs. It prepares preschool children for the next leg of their journey. Time-outs should be thought of as a time to calm down and recompose, not as punishment. Time-outs are best when thought of as a time away from overstimulation and negative interactions. Children can go to a quiet place and return when they are calmer.

Families continue to be a major source of socialization for preschool children. Alfred Adler emphasized the importance of family decades ago (Dreikurs 1953), and proof of this remains, as witnessed by the research of Gesell Institute and others over the years. For decades, the Gesell Institute has promoted the importance of understanding a child's development and involvement in the family as the entire family travels the journey together (Gesell and Ilg 1955). Dr. Burton White and his associates stressed that the family can be influential to the outcome of the child. Family interactions continue to provide groundwork for how children will relate to others in the future. Siblings stimulate each other, and the interactions will contrast between positive and negative. Siblings and peers begin to notice strengths and weaknesses in each other (White 1975, 1995). It is frustrating for parents as their children struggle to find ways of relating to others, especially in the family.

Parallel play, when children play alongside each other, is prominent during the toddler and preschool years. Parallel play begins to decrease during the preschool years, and children become more interactive, showing more interest in other people. As their interaction with others increases, they participate in sharing, taking turns, and interactional play. With maturity, attention span continues to increase.

Preschool children may become interested in making up their own games, which shows their evolving initiative. Part of healthy development is learning to respect other people, even though they may be different from us. Children need to develop respect to live within a family and community and function within social guidelines. Preschool children are beginning to notice differences in various cultures of family and community. They are more aware of the differences in others. As preschool children become more involved in activities away from the family, and they show increased interest in playing with other children, parents may begin to hear "... does it this way," "... gets to stay up later than me," "At ... house, they watch TV while they eat," and on and on. The best way to respond is "Every family does things a little differently." Gradually, they begin to understand that people are different and have different ways of doing things.

As we follow the growth and development of children and our growth as parents, we can see the validity of the work of Alfred Adler and his associates/followers, as they asserted that life is a continuous process of past, present, and future. Adler's humanistic growth model demonstrates the importance of childhood experiences. This model also shows that people can change and grow with positive encouragement. If we reflect on our parenting years, we see that a balance between work and play is important, even though we may feel like we are always struggling to maintain a healthy balance.

As we have followed the progression from infants through toddler and preschool stages, we have seen proof of the social learning theory as we observed the parts that imagination and imitation play. We have seen the congruence of Erikson's theory and Piaget's theory with the social learning theory. We have recognized the consistency of temperament from three to four years of age, to five and six. As preschool children approach the next stage of development, we begin to notice some maturity in their thinking and actions. As children pass to the next developmental stage, we witness them continuing to establish their identity and sense of self.

Relationships are not static. The dynamics of the parent child-relationship change as children evolve. Quality time and unconditional love continue to strengthen the foundation. Love and nurturing will set the stage for future relationships and life choices as children move toward gradual independence.

This Is My Child

While doing the following activity, think about your child and what he or she likes to do. This activity will give you the opportunity to think about your child as a unique individual and will give you insight to your child's likes and dislikes, strengths and weaknesses.

1. My child prefers outdoor play, *or* indoor play .
2. My child prefers active games (running, climbing, jumping), *or* quiet games (books, coloring, puzzles).
3. My child prefers looking at books or watching videos, **or** doing puzzles, coloring, *or* building with Legos.

4. My child prefers coloring, or building with blocks.
5. My child prefers to listen to a story on a CD, *or* sit quietly and look at a book.
6. My child prefers water play, *or* my child prefers to play in a sandbox.
7. My child's favorite thing to do alone is: _____.
8. My child's favorite thing to do with me alone is: _____.
9. My child's favorite book is: _____.
10. The thing my child and I do together the most is: _____.
11. My child is happiest when: _____.
12. The thing that my child dislikes the most is: _____.
13. My child's fear is: _____.
14. My favorite thing to do with my child is: _____.
15. My child frequently talks about his/her day or feelings _____, *or* my child does not talk openly about feelings and events but appears to quietly observe what is going on around him/herself, and at a later date reveals things, which leads me to believe that he/she is very observant _____.

Designed by Linda Powers, RN, BS and Heather Ramer, BA (copyright 1996, 2004).

This activity is designed to help you understand the child. This is not to be used as a formal assessment tool or evaluation.

Chapter 5

Latency: The School Age Child—A Time for Learning and Assimilating

Latency, which covers a longer span than the preceding stages of infancy, toddler, and preschool, may feel like a breath of calmness. Sandwiched between the energetic toddler and preschool years and the tumultuous teens, latency can be a less chaotic time; a time of optimism and hope. After the amazing changes during preschool development, children seem more mature as they approach five to six years of age, the beginning of the elementary school years. They carry on mutual conversations more easily and they begin to show more logic. They demonstrate increased attention span, more independence, and more interest in interactive play, and they are slowly beginning to understand the point of view of others.

Children are assimilating all that they are learning

academically, cognitively, socially, culturally, and morally. Entering the latency stage, they are ready for more focused learning. They spend less time within the core of the family as they participate in more peer and community activities, with less parental supervision. Although they do not require the constant supervision of a toddler or preschooler, they continue to need parental guidance. At times, they may act as though family is not as important as it once was, but the nurturing family environment continues to hold love and security for children while they continue on their journey toward healthy interdependence.

Children in latency are becoming aware that they are multidimensional; they realize that each person is an individual, and at the same time a person fills many roles. A young girl understands, for example, that she is a daughter, a granddaughter, a niece, a friend, a classmate, a student, maybe a sister, possibly a member of a sports team, a member of chorus or band, and many other roles, all while being herself. Development of a sense of being an individual who fulfills multiple roles in a healthy way can occur with ordinary, everyday activities. Children can be encouraged to mingle with their friends, remember the birthday of a family member, complete their homework for the following Monday, and engage in their team swim meet. A variety of activities, emphasizing enjoyment and mastery of skill rather than unhealthy competition, contribute to development and skills.

Children are drawn to activities in which they excel, and they can use their strengths to build their competencies. At the same time, children may use every excuse they can think of to not participate in their weaker areas. It can be a tricky balance to encourage children in their strong points while at the same time strategizing to provide opportunities for them to strengthen weak areas. A child who excels at sports and does well in reading and language arts may balk at math, an individual weak area. Finding the balance may take trial and error on the parts of the child, parent, and teachers.

Within a family, children might differ in their interests or have similar interests. My daughters all loved dancing and swimming and were accomplished at both, taking their talents to different lengths. Two participated on a swim team; two became lifeguards and swim instructors. All were at ease in the dance classroom and in productions. One of my daughter's interests in sports extended to playing softball and volleyball. They all had the opportunity for music lessons, and my youngest daughter maintained her interest in piano the longest. They could share their common interests, yet each one had her individual interest to pursue.

Sometimes we notice strengths in our children that can be nurtured into qualities that serve them well as adults. My youngest daughter showed traits of being an educator early on. As a child, she loved playing school as she arranged her dolls in a pretend classroom. Her mannerisms portrayed an interest in education and teaching others, but I was careful to not focus on this, concerned that it would diminish her interest. She continued to play school beyond the usual age, but I let it happen as a way to encourage what I witnessed as one of her strengths. Even though she reverted to a type of play commonly associated with a younger age, teaching her dolls as she did her homework, I continued to observe a balance. One hour later, she was functioning at socially appropriate levels with her peers; two hours later, as an avid reader, she engaged in reading at a level that was advanced for her grade level. Variation in each child, and in different children within the same peer group, or the same family, is always interesting.

During the elementary school years, children learn the importance of productivity, realizing that industry and accomplishment are important in the world. Through school and other activities, they are industrious, learning that effort and patience reap rewards, although they may need reminders about patience. As development continues, they continue to acquire knowledge and abilities rapidly. Acquiring new skills, they build a sense of competence. They may not admit that the academic part of learning is fun, and few children see school as the opportunity to gain knowledge, but watching children of this age, one can see how they thrive on learning new things. Children show individual characteristics in the way they learn and processes information.

Erikson identified the developmental task of this stage as *industry* versus *inferiority*. Industry is obvious as the child strives to master tasks, academically, cognitively, socially, personally, and physically. Erikson defined *competence* as the strength attained through industry and successful application of work. Self-satisfaction and pride accompany competence. Erikson believed that a child who has not achieved competence through industry experiences a general feeling of inferiority, resulting in a lack of motivation and *inertia*. Inferiority, when children experience a low self-image or poor self-worth, may cause them to feel that they can do nothing right. They may feel put down as they compare themselves to others or fear that they are being compared with others. They might feel that they cannot get ahead or accomplish anything successfully. Inferiority can encompass failure, and the resulting inertia can threaten to halt the ability of the child to move forward. Inferiority can also result in a child being overly competitive, or unwilling to compete at all. As in previous stages of development, regression normally occurs during transition times, development changes, fatigue, or stress and is usually temporary. Regression that may follow the general sense of inferiority can be encompassing and more difficult to come out of. Approaches that help in these times are validation, gentleness, love, and nurturing.

As they develop and have diversified interests, latency age children become well rounded and versatile. They are learning socially. They try new things and discover what they like and dislike. They make their preferences and dislikes known. Strengths are more evident as they try a variety of activities and realize the power of mastering a task. During this stage, it is important to continue nurturing talents and strengths, while at the same time offering opportunities to strengthen weaknesses. Children who are easily distracted may need help mastering skills to help them focus better. Some children need guidance in managing impulsivity or anxiety.

During latency, as in infancy, toddlerhood, and

the preschool years, all areas of development (physical, cognitive, social, language, moral, emotional, spiritual, moral, and sexual) continue as they integrate to form the whole individual. Cognitive changes are evident in their approach to problem solving, and emotional ups and downs become more prevalent as adolescence approaches. Sexual development moves ahead near the end of this stage. Through developmental gains, they acquire mastery over more tasks. Each child has an individual timetable of development, and variations are observable.

Temperament remains consistent, and some personality characteristics may be more pronounced. Depending on individual temperament, children respond differently to discipline. Parents and caregivers find it beneficial to keep the individual temperaments in mind with their approaches to guidance, learning, and discipline. The shy introvert may need encouragement in participating in social and group activities. The sensitive child may be more easily stimulated or anxious with novel experiences or emotional situations, and might respond to discipline with an exaggerated response. The hyperactive, distracted child will move quickly and intensely from one activity to another. The more reactive child may seem more difficult to handle, presenting more of a challenge, stubbornly resisting corrections and guidance (discipline).

As gross and fine motor coordination are improving, many tasks become easier. Yet there will be children who display clumsiness in some areas, and some children may seem to be accident-prone. Encouraging them to slow down a little may be helpful. Children benefit from proper rest and sleep, along with nutrition, exercise, and downtime. As the ones guiding their development, we can encourage healthy lifestyles.

Encouraging children to ask questions helps them consider their thoughts as they formulate their answers. Guide them to resources to find the answers. If an adult does not know an answer, the best response is, "I do not know, but I think this is where we can find an answer." This encourages them to look for the answers, helping them feel productive and helpful. Watching television or movies together, answer questions and encourage discussion to make sure children are receiving the message they should. At various times, we found children's magazines, such as *Highlights for Children, Consumer Reports for Children,* or *Kids' National Geographic,* good tools for learning while having fun. Kitchen experiments were fun, and I remember making our own soda using juice and soda water, following directions in one issue of *Consumer Reports for Children.*

As during their earlier developmental years, children of this age observe everything in their world around them. They usually take in far more than we realize. Some children may be observers and may not talk about what they have observed, but will randomly show their observations with related questions at a later time. Other children will readily talk about their observations. Each child is unique in expressing individual observations, which may vary with the circumstances. Sometimes it will be matter of fact or a simple question; other times, the statement or question may provide a hint of deeper insight and observations. Recently, I was watching the movie *Elf* with my nine-year-old grandson, Ben. About halfway through the movie, he looked at me and asked, "Mammie, will he ever become more mature?" My response was "Not necessarily. Why do you ask?" His response—"Just wondered." Trying hard not to smile, I realized the detail of his observations, but he was not giving me a clue as to what specific observations he made. I was left to contemplate the insight of a nine-year-old who a few hours previously had been running around, laughing, and being silly with his younger brother.

Imagination continues to be active, more so in some children than others. This often leads to creativity with projects or play. One of my daughters took multiple pretend trips to many places around the world, in her pretend vehicle. It was amazing how quickly she could return from a kangaroo-searching trip to Australia (less than three minutes) when one of her favorite foods was being served for dinner. On the other hand, one of her trips to Boston to pick up someone at the airport could last a very long time if she was procrastinating, avoiding something she did not want to do. There would be multiple stops along the way to let people off or get gas—until her parents approached their patience limit.

Games can be the highlight of a day, and games become more elaborate. Children are capable of following directions, and as time passes, they need fewer explanations. They enjoy making up their own games or changing the rules of a standard game, showing their creativity. As children create their own rules, they may be accused of cheating. As the adults in charge, we need to be aware of our own attitudes and ideas about cheating and rules so we can help them understand when it's okay to adjust the rules and when it's not okay to improvise.

Play, which is now more productive and focused, continues to be an important part of learning. Their interactive play is sometimes based on reality, and other times leans toward the magical or fantasy/fiction side. Play is a way for them to try out many different roles and see which ones are comfortable or not comfortable. Having observed work and personal ethics in those around them, they may incorporate these into their play. Electronics are a common draw to kids today, but the old-fashioned board games and card games play a major role in cognitive, language, cultural, social, and moral development. Healthy competition during a board game or card game can be a lifelong lesson that benefits children for years to come. Math, spelling, and word games provide entertainment and challenges and promote cognitive skills. Puzzles improve visual-spatial coordination.

Through experiences and observation, they learn cultural and social guidelines and expectations. Fun activities make learning a positive experience as interest expands to different cultures and customs. A fun activity our family enjoyed one summer was preparing different meals from different countries. Each week, one of the girls would pick a country of interest to her, and we would learn a little bit about the country, including favorite foods. On a given day, each girl, with adult guidance, would prepare a simple meal from that country. This encouraged learning about other cultures and enlarged their world.

Children wonder about family traditions and may

search for differences in their families. As they learn about different countries and traditions, it is not unusual for them to want to incorporate new ideas into their own lives. In fifth grade, my middle daughter had to write a paper on a country that one of her ancestors originated from. She was hoping to discover an ancestor from France. In the late 1880's my maternal grandfather's parents had come to the United States from Wales and England but my daughter thought these countries were boring. My mother-in-law's parents had come from Germany, but even that did not satisfy my daughter's search for French ancestors. She called both her grandmothers, asking if they were sure none of our ancestors came from France, and she was disappointed in their responses. It was around this time that talks were occurring about tearing down the wall between East and West Berlin, and my daughter professed an interest in the conflict and what was going to be done to resolve it. She finally chose Germany as the country to write about but reminded us all many times that she wished she had ancestors from France.

Sometimes, latency-age children engage in activities designed for younger children. This is okay, as it helps reinforce their sense of mastery in an area and provides comfort they may need. Other times, they may feel confident and ready to attempt new experiences. Many children continue to have a favorite stuffed animal, blanket, or other love object for bedtime or when they need comforting and security. This is fine. By this time, they have given up the need to take it with them, but it is a source of comfort, waiting for them in their rooms when they need it. Gradually, dependence on the object can be weaned, as a child is ready.

Reading to themselves, or aloud with a parent or caregiver, is an enriching experience for all involved, as the participants use imagination while discussing different aspects of the story. Arts and crafts provide self-expression for the developing mind. Before the days of computers and tablets, which self-instruct, many children followed along in a book as they listened to an audiotape of someone reading the book. Today, with so many video games and other electronics, unfortunately, children may not have the opportunity to engage in creative writing as often. Children can write or journal with words or pictures to express themselves, or as a means of communication with others.

Latency is a time when children are drawn to collections and proudly display their accomplishments. They may enthusiastically dive into a project they're interested in while procrastinating and resisting school-assigned projects or home-based chores. They have learned to win recognition for their accomplishments and are enjoying it, promoting a sense of industry and productivity as they apply themselves to tasks. Interest in specific tasks and projects may be consistent or may rapidly change.

Peer acceptance is important. While they are realizing more and more that they are individuals, unique in time and space, they also strive to be like their peers. Friends are of prime importance. Latency age children, especially pre-teens, may be preoccupied with finding friends and impressing the right people. Friends may change from day to day, especially among girls. They compare themselves to others, especially peers. Children pay even more attention to the different ways other families do things and the different rules and expectations among their peers. As mentioned previously, I find the best response is a simple explanation that different families have different rules, expectations, and ways of doing things. Children are always concerned about the fairness to them and are quick to point out that a peer has more freedom. I often said, "We are doing what seems to work best for us at this time." There is always room for negotiation, but anything concerning safety should not be negotiable. Parents are still in charge and set the guidelines. If parents have certain preferences, like Sunday dinner should be a family occasion; no cell phones at the dinner table, or television should be turned off during a meal, I believe it is respectful for the child to adjust and follow these requests. Negotiations may be helpful in promoting harmony if there are differences of opinions. As they strive to become more independent, children learn that independence is earned as they show developmental readiness. Some children show more insight and maturity than others, while some are impulsive and need more guidance. Some children are more histrionic, or dramatic, than others, making each little thing a major event in their life. This child will need more guidance in understanding the difference between reality and fiction.

Groups and clubs are a norm for this age group. One thing that makes groups intriguing is having secret rules. Unfortunately, this can encourage cliques and sometimes pettiness. For this reason, adults should monitor the overall group to discourage peer discrimination. This is a good time to discuss being fair and respectful to all people, even if they are different from us, and not being exclusively loyal to the group at the cost of disrespect or discrimination. Kids of this age can sometimes be bossy, argumentative, and opinionated. This is part of social learning, and they may need some adult guidance. Gender difference is more noticeable as girls gravitate to other girls and may express disinterest in boys. The same is true of the attitudes of boys toward girls at this time.

Children enjoy structured group activities led by a capable adult, like scouts, sports, after-school programs, or church youth programs. Sports offer an opportunity for children to be part of the team. While a certain amount of competition is healthy, sometimes the competition can go overboard, pressuring the kids to win and accomplish, with little regard for the healthy part of enjoying the comradeship and team experience. This psychological pressure is not healthy. Children in latency may resist adult guidance, but they still need the supervision to maintain a fair and appropriate social-peer environment. Awareness of the feelings of others progresses as children gain more empathy. Children learn empathy, as well as prejudice, by example and experience.

School presents a culture of its own with rules, regulations, and expectations. Some children may struggle to meet academic or social expectations. Doing their own homework is part of accepting responsibility for themselves. It is okay to check it over, but do not do it for them. If they do not complete assignments, they need to accept the consequences. Learning through mistakes due to lack of understanding, or rushing, provides important life lessons. Helping them prioritize and organize is a great gift you can offer. Most teachers welcome parent-teacher communication, and good communication is one of the keys to successful education.

It is common for children and adolescents to complain that school, or even life, feel boring. Giving an appropriate response is challenging. We may be tempted to remind them that if they are bored, they should improve their academics or help with more chores. I have often thought that kids get in the habit of saying they are bored, and continue to say it, maybe without meaning. Sometimes it is best to ignore this common complaint; other times, it might be worth a discussion to find out specifically why they are bored and what they could do to change this.

Different children have different patterns for doing homework assignments and projects. Some can sustain attention to tasks while sitting at the kitchen table with a sibling while a parent is preparing dinner. Another child will be easily distracted in this setting. Some children need a quiet, undisturbed place, always in the same room, at the same desk. Others feel bored if confined to one space repeatedly and need to find various places to complete different assignments. One of my daughters was like this, needing to move from one location to another, depending on what the assignment was. Sometimes it was the kitchen table; other times it might be her room; at other times, it might be at the desk in the den, where it was quiet. At times, this made it challenging for the rest of the family, but we all adapted and survived.

Children within the same family vary in educational levels and achievements. As with other areas, focus on the individual's need; encourage strengths and provide ways to help a child strengthen weaknesses. Some children will excel in math; others will be reading at levels beyond their academic years; some may migrate with an interest toward science. As time passes, some may develop an interest in history, social studies, or other cultures. Work with this. Respect the differences, knowing that each child will contribute to the world in a unique way.

As educational levels and interests vary, internal motivation varies too. Some children are internally motivated to achieve with minimal acknowledgment from adults; others may need guiding steps along the way, accomplishing small steps one at a time, until the final goal is reached. My daughters differed in their approaches. One responded best to having contracts with identified small steps to meet the goal. My middle daughter found reviewing for spelling tests and doing repetitive homework assignments tedious. She wanted to have goldfish, and we used this as an incentive to motivate her. My husband drew a picture of a fish on a large piece of graph paper, and we placed it on the front of the refrigerator, in view as a reminder. For each spelling test grade and each homework assignment completed, she could color in a determined number of squares. For example, if she earned a 90 on a spelling test, she could color in 9 small squares. When the drawing of the fish was completed, she went to the pet store with her dad and got four goldfish, an aquarium, and the required setup. She was proud of her fish, as she watched them and fed them and helped (although not enthusiastically) to clean the tank. Very attached to her fish, she named them Fred, Frieda, Pat, and Carol. After several months of doing well, they succumbed to fish heaven, one at a time. This was her first real experience with grieving. What I found interesting was that one died on Holy Thursday, one on Good Friday, and the third on Easter Sunday. I have always wondered if there was some hidden meaning in this but I never figured out the answer. Frieda, the fourth fish, lived for several more weeks and then passed. After saying a prayer for Frieda, my daughter, at the time a third grader, decided to write a book and dedicate it to Frieda. This act seemed to ease her sadness, and we moved on to other things.

Accepting responsibility and doing age-appropriate chores contribute to a sense of individual competence and offers the benefit of family teamwork. Chores are a part of learning and growing. As much as they might grumble and complain, children in this stage are capable of assuming some responsibility for themselves, like making their beds, picking up their rooms, placing dirty clothes in the designated spot, helping set or clear the table, picking up games and activities, or taking out the garbage. No, you will not find hospital corners when your children make their beds, but if they neaten the bed and pull up the comforter, there is a semblance of a made bed and they are assuming responsibility. They may not clean their room as thoroughly as you would, and you might find yourself attacking their room to clean and organize to your own expectations, but children can be responsible for some degree of neatness. Beware—reminding is usually needed. One thing that worked for us was writing down appropriate chores on small pieces of paper and placing them in a bowl. Each child picked one or two chores from the bowl. This way, the children chose chores randomly and there were fewer chances for alleged favoritism. Children often complain that a parent "nags all the time." I have told many children, "Do you know you have control over helping your parent stop nagging? What do you think you could do to make that happen?" Sometimes, I get a blank look, and then the light dawns, and they reply, "Just do it the first time."

Some children, especially the hyperactive, are easily distractible. Someone with ADHD, or a child with sensory or motor problems, will respond best to simple directions. For example, if the following list of requests is made, "Please eat your breakfast, brush your teeth, get your backpack, and put on your jacket because it is almost time to leave for school," the child who is easily distracted or who has a short attention span might hear only the first and last requests. The child is already distracted and has trouble following multiple requests. It works best to make one request at a time, after a previous step has been completed. This can be tedious for the parent or caregiver, but it is helpful. Eventually, over time, the child will learn the routine. A chart can serve as a reminder, listing the morning activities, after-school routine, or bedtime routine. Children can be reminded to check their list if they forget to do something or are distracted. A list of words for the child who can read is simple to do. For the child who is not yet reading, pictures work well. This encourages children to take responsibility for themselves. If children participate in making the chart, this gives some ownership and pride, and the routine is incorporated into their memory.

Contracts are helpful. They may be verbal or written. Written contracts offer more formality, sometimes making more of an impression. An example of a contract would be that if they can keep their room neat for four out of seven days a week, they earn a reward. Another contract might be about verbal expression of feelings. Children can earn a checkmark or a star each time they use words and appropriate ways to express their anger and frustration. After a determined number of stars or checkmarks, an agreed-upon reward is earned. Rewards do not have to be monetary. In fact, monetary rewards stress the importance of money and gifts, which is not always a good message. When money and gifts are involved, the child may begin to consider money and gifts as more important than pride and accomplishment, and focus on the task at hand diminishes. Examples of nonmonetary rewards: the child can choose a special meal or dessert; or the child can earn the privilege of staying up later on a night when there is no school the next day. Extra one-on-one time with a parent or favorite adult is another reward that both adult and child can enjoy.

Like the chart to encourage the accomplishment of routines, the chart for a contract can take effort to draw up and maintain. But it is worth it. Certain behaviors, if practiced enough, become automatic habits, and then the child easily performs the expected chores without needing positive reinforcement and concrete rewards. It becomes part of their routine. Try practice runs on weekends and on school breaks. If we, as parents and caretakers, can make the busy mornings easier, it is worth it. This may be a hard place to get to, but once there, life is smoother. Respect is an important part of disciplining; the purpose is to teach and guide so the child learns a lesson. Respect the developmental level and age so that the child can process and understand the consequence.

Grounding is a common means of discipline. It means different things to different people. I always advise that one should consider the effects of a consequence on both the child and parent (or person enforcing the consequence). In anger or frustration, an adult may react and tell the child he is grounded for two months. If one stops to think about it logically, what are the circumstances for grounding, and how does it impact family or classroom functioning? What can the child learn from the grounding experience? Discipline, teaching and guiding, should be the point of any consequence. Expecting a ten-year-old to stay in a room for two months, except for school and meals, is highly unrealistic. I prefer, and recommend, removing privileges as a consequence. Privileges are earned, just as independence is earned. One can have a privilege when one has demonstrated the ability to appropriately and safely use, or apply, the privilege. Removing electronic privileges is a common consequence, either removing all electronic privileges, including phone (if they have their own), television, and video games, or removing one electronic activity, with the understanding that another can be removed if needed. Another privilege to remove is a fun activity, like a sleepover, a fun day with a friend, or a fun activity. Set a limit but offer the child the opportunity to earn back the privilege through good behavior and respect for a reasonable amount of time. This is when we really see the benefits of consistency. It is normal for kids to push the limit, but if there is consistency, they quickly realize their pushing is ineffective. Parents should not give consequences until their anger and frustration have subsided and they feel ready to discipline and teach in a calm manner. Consequences that occur from anger in the heat of the moment are more like punishments than learning experiences.

Time-outs are another common consequence. Time-outs should be time for children to regain composure and reflect on their actions. It should not be thought of as a punishment. Time-outs can be in a quiet room or the corner of a room, where there is little opportunity for interaction or stimulation. Afterward, the reason for the time-out and the behavior should be calmly discussed. Avoid lecturing. Meet the child at an individual level and talk in a clear but brief way.

Early on, children should learn the value of time alone to rest and reflect. Being in constant motion is not good for anyone, and all children need to realize that. My daughters moaned and groaned because in the summer, if there were no structured activities scheduled for after lunch, we had an hour of quiet time. During this time, children were asked to be on different floors of the house, or in separate rooms, for quiet time, with no interaction between them. The original purpose of this was to save my sanity on the long summer days and decrease the likelihood of sibling arguing. We had many tents built under the dining room table or kitchen table. Workstations were set up in the family room or a bedroom to accomplish an arts and crafts project. Reading was accomplished. Despite their moaning and groaning, everyone survived, and each one of us gained some time to think and reflect. I fully realized the success of this intervention when, one by one, each of my daughters began to babysit, returning home saying, "Mom, now I know why we had quiet time."

Truth and honesty are important to stress in everyday living, not only when the child does something wrong. Many children will attempt stealing, either on a dare or to see how much they can get away with. They should be held accountable for stealing and receive consequences appropriate for the offense. What is the best way to deal with lying? It is not effective to confront the children and accuse them of lying. That can come back to slap us in the face as the child becomes defensive and even more determined to not open up. It helps to say something like, "I am getting the feeling you may not be telling the truth" or, "I am getting the feeling something's not right here." Or "I am thinking we need to discuss this a little more because I just do not understand." You are giving the child the chance to save face.

Structure and consistency in the environment continue to provide security for children, as they know what to expect. Discipline, guidance, love, and a structured environment remain priorities as children continue to try out what they have learned, experienced, or observed in their environment. Emotional rapport as a foundation for discipline is as important now as it was with the toddler and preschooler. At this stage, the child is better able to understand consequences, whether the consequences are positive or negative. Safety and respect remain crucial in discipline as the environment changes to adapt to the latency-age child, allowing more appropriate freedom and decisions.

It is the right of the parent, or the adult in charge, to oversee electronic activities for safety, appropriateness, and time. The American Academy of Pediatrics recommends that parents maintain a "healthy media diet, limiting and overseeing electronics while teaching children how to appropriately and safely use technology tools." Too much time with electronics can be unhealthy because it reduces the opportunity for social interactions, physical activity, hands-on exploration, and adequate sleep. Dr. Gary Small, in his book *i Brain* (2008), reminds that digital stimulation teaches a faster response time, and because the messages are encoded into the brain differently than in traditional learning, there is a shorter attention span than with traditional forms of learning. Dr. Small also states that overuse of electronics can overwhelm the neural circuits in the developing brain of the child. With too much brain stimulation, a person can experience anxiety, distractibility, decreased attention span, hyperactivity, irritability, or decreased self-esteem. Brains do not function well with too much stimulation. The American Academy of Pediatrics suggests having ongoing communication with children about online guidelines for safety, along with delegating media-free areas in the home. Many latency children are involved in educational games such as Minecraft. The American Academy of Pediatrics suggests that parents and children share the activities of these educational games as a way of monitoring and connecting with each other. Watching a TV show or movie with your child and discussing it provides a learning experience and offers different ways of looking at situations. As with the preschooler, pointing out reality versus fiction plays an important part in cognitive, emotional, and social development. (For more information on media and children, go to the American Academy of Pediatrics website, https://www.aap.org/en-us/Pages/Default.aspx.)

Criticism needs to be clear and realistic, at the same time pointing out strengths and helping the child find a way to improve a weakness. Children are sensitive to criticism, even if they present a tough exterior. Too much faultfinding and criticism can lead to children thinking they are inferior and unable to meet expectations. Soon, the feeling of inferiority may extend from one area to another. Although they may try to hide it, children are easily embarrassed or discouraged. They also can be unnecessarily self-critical. Working through this with gentle encouragement and guidance, taking into account the temperament of the individual child, provides the most effective strategy.

The child moves from the preoperational stage of cognitive development to the operational stage around the age of six or seven years. This stage continues through eleven or twelve years of age, or later. The operational stage is a major turning point in cognitive development because it marks the beginning of logical and concrete thought. In what Piaget defined as the operational stage, children are more proficient in their logical thought and realistic thinking. Like other developmental stages, the chronological age of onset varies from child to child, depending on inherent characteristics, environment, and culture. During the operational stage, children gain abilities of conservation, such as understanding that something may stay the same quantity if appearance changes. They realize that when six ounces of water are poured from a short wide glass to a taller thin glass, which holds twelve ounces, the quantity of water remains the same—six ounces. Concepts become more general and realistic. Attention is more focused and selective; they can tune into what they consider more important. They gain understanding of numbers, area, length, volume, orientation, and reversibility. They more easily identify groups and categories and can mentally arrange items according to hierarchy. Their understanding of space and distance is more realistic. They show ability to solve problems in a logical and concrete way, although they are not capable of thinking abstractly or hypothetically. As the operational stage comes to a close, the child may display the beginning of abstract thinking.

Through experience, the child is internalizing right and wrong, and the conscience continues to develop. Kohlberg asserted that latency-age children remain at the preconventional level of moral development, making decisions based on what benefits them and avoids punishment. They are more likely to follow rules imposed by an adult authority figure but may be tempted to disobey if they think they might not be caught. Approaching mid to late latency, children may progress to the beginning of the conventional level as they begin to understand the needs and feelings of others, and how others may be affected by behavior and consequences. They begin to focus more on mutual satisfaction of needs and define right and wrong based on how the event impacts them and others they are closely affiliated with. They continue to want to please others and try to be good according to social norms, law, and order.

Feelings and emotions are part of who we are and are not right or wrong. The way we express our feelings can be appropriate or inappropriate. Encourage children to express their emotions appropriately. It is okay to feel angry, but yelling, screaming, hitting, and being mean are not okay. Children can learn to use their words to express their anger. For example, it is okay to say, "I feel mad, but I do not know why." Then the problem solving can begin with dialogue between child and adult. Children need to feel comfortable expressing their feelings and know that it is not healthy to repress emotions. Children of this age may have worries and may be reluctant to express these worries verbally. They may fear that expressing worries or anxieties makes them a failure. It is important for children to understand that everyone experiences anxieties about certain things, especially anything new. Children can learn healthy ways to express concerns and worries and develop skills to manage their worries so their functioning is not impacted.

Validation is an important part of healthy communication and healthy emotion. We all want to be heard. Validating is acknowledging what you heard someone say or do; it is not agreeing with or condoning the verbal message or the behavior. In validating, you are acknowledging that you heard what was said, and you are recognizing the emotions involved. Validation and feedback encourage the formation of identity and self-worth in everyone, whether adult or child. An example might be that your ten-year-old wants to go to the movies alone with a friend and you do not believe this is appropriate for your child. Your child begins to argue and say things like "You always treat me like such a baby. I am not a baby!" A helpful response might be, "I know you may feel like I am treating you like a baby. You are my daughter who is growing up fast. But I am concerned about you being in the movie theater alone with a friend in the city. Unfortunately, there are some people who might be disrespectful of children and try to take advantage of them in many ways. I want you and your friend to be safe." Maybe you can negotiate a plan that would work for all concerned. Maybe you could offer to accompany the children to the movies and sit several rows behind them, where you can observe them and be sure they are safe and behaving appropriately.

Examples of role models, whether real or mythical, imagined or fictional, predominate in the mind of children as they assimilate and process. With parents and other adults as constant role models in reality, children learn appropriate behavior through observation and experience. Although we may be angry and frustrated with our children at times, they should be treated with respect. They are humans, not objects. Experiencing and observing respect assists them in their treatment of others. They may remember how they felt in response to certain situations more than remembering the event itself. Respectful communication is part of guiding your child toward healthy interdependence.

Children continue to need their families for security, stability, and guidance. Family interactions and activities continue to be a large part of molding the child. Through these activities, the concepts of respect and sharing are reinforced. Family interactions impact future relationships. As a way of decreasing the commercialism around Christmas, our family exchanged names and had secret friends. A few weeks before Christmas, each family member would pick a name of another family member. Each person had to secretly do something nice for the secret friend, such as sneak in and make the person's bed, lie out pajamas before bedtime, or perform another thoughtful act. It never took long before each person guessed the identity of the secret friend, and then we would exchange names again. This frequent exchanging of names kept interest piqued and kept the game alive.

Avoid comparison of children. The family is a team and operates as one, with everyone sharing responsibility. Ongoing sibling rivalry and competition need our watchful eye, although we cannot prevent it. Looking forward to one-on-one time alone with a parent or other trusted caregiver promotes the self-worth of all children.

Helping our children adapt to changes in life is our priority. Consider the whole child, along with overall development and temperament. We all may regress with fatigue, insecurity, stress, illness, or transitions. We all need the security of familiarity. As we watch children develop, it is amazing to see their sense of industry and competency progress while they adapt to the world through learning, observing, playing, and experiencing. We witness them developing mind-sets. Respect each child for individual uniqueness. Each child's unique traits should be nurtured.

Parenting is a career, and like all careers, it has its ups and downs. There are times when it is easy to feel the joy of parenting and the blessings that children bring to our lives. The frustrations, the overwhelming list of things to do and oversee, and the daunting task of providing an environment in which our children thrive, can feel insurmountable at times. Getting through these times can be tough and tiring. When we make a mistake, react too quickly, or do not understand where the child is coming from, we need to be honest with the child. Honesty and genuineness teach children many things about life and interactions with others.

When we are enmeshed in parts of the parenting journey, it can feel like forever. But overall, time passes quickly. As children move from one stage to another, some stages are difficult, and some are easier. Look for the positive. Sometimes you have to look harder, but there is always a beacon of light glowing like a star to guide us, even among fatigue and frustration. Years later, we will be amazed at how fast the time passed during the latency years, and during the teen years, we may even yearn for the calmer, latency years.

As a grandparent of five wonderful kids at various stages of development, I have enjoyed watching them every step of the way. Each one is different, yet I see similar characteristics and some traits of their parents.

Nurturing and loving remain the keys for approaching the next developmental stage in a positive way. Enjoy the latency years as your child gains more independence and continues to build on their foundation.

Chapter 6

Adolescence: The Struggle of Identity

Adolescence spans the years from latency to young adulthood. It is often referred to as the bridge between childhood and adulthood. The beginning and end of adolescence are not marked by specific chronological ages, as this time period varies among individuals, depending on physical, emotional, social, and cognitive development. However, the general age span is from eleven or thirteen to eighteen or twenty. Adolescence embodies the accrued experiences of childhood and is the integration of emotional, learning, and relationship experiences with previous play experiences. Each adolescent struggles to establish an identity and discover who the real person is.

Most laws recognize anyone eighteen or over as adults, allowing them to partake of adult privileges, such as living on their own, voting, buying cigarettes, and serving in the military, not to mention sexual freedom. Research shows that full maturity of the brain is not established until the middle twenties, and in some cases the thirties. MRI studies of brain functioning have confirmed that the brain does not fully mature in both males and females until this time, and the female brain tends to develop about two years earlier than the male brain. This has raised the question if eighteen-year-olds are mature and responsible enough to make well-thought-out decisions.

Significant brain growth is a process, continuing from the age of eighteen to the mid-twenties, or when brain maturity is attained. The last part of the brain to develop is the prefrontal cortex, which is the part of the brain involved in decision-making, thinking, planning, organizing, complex problem solving, and communicating. This part of the brain also controls impulses, and if not fully developed, can contribute to a person engaging in riskier behaviors and making impulsive decisions. Therefore, adolescents may react impulsively because messages are coming from the amygdala, which is the part of the brain involved with emotions. Since the immature prefrontal cortex limits judgment, the adolescents' impulsive reactions from the amygdala bring instant gratification, and the cost can be the unnecessary risk of impaired decisions. In addition, the immature, adolescent brain is more vulnerable to addiction than the adult brain, raising concern among professionals. During puberty, as the brain matures, it prunes, or trims, excess connections of synapses. All behavior and experiences up to age twenty-five, or the time when the brain is mature, have the potential to affect the brain. As the prefrontal cortex matures, a person gains insight and is able to better understand consequences associated with actions. Clearer insight also allows the adult brain to better understand the perspective of another person. Communication skills and executive functioning improve as the brain matures, and peer pressure is of less importance.

Development of the prefrontal cortex is gradual and not always consistent. One minute the adolescent acts in a mature manner, using insight and rational thinking. At other moments, they revert to concrete and less insightful thinking, which may appear to be at the level of a younger child. This is all part of the process as adolescents move toward adulthood.

As they move through adolescence, and the frontal lobe continues to develop, young people begin to move into Piaget's formal operational stage of cognitive development. Their thinking shifts from concrete to more abstract. Because the brain is not fully mature, adolescents may quickly revert to more immature thinking and decisions, alternating with abstract and mature thinking. To prepare adolescents for life, it is helpful if they are allowed to take healthy risks to learn the consequences of their actions. Healthy risks, overseen by mature adults, contribute to the sense of identity in the adolescent, and the adolescents feel that that they have some control over their life and decisions.

The main task of adolescents is to become psychologically emancipated from their parents. Adolescents will distance themselves from their parents, shown with rebellion or questioning of parental thoughts and values. Adolescents must go through this distancing before they can relate to their parents from an adult perspective. Each individual goes through the distancing a little differently. Parents also move through the emancipation process, gradually distancing themselves from their adolescents. This natural process is necessary for individuation to be accomplished. Adolescents gradually rely less on parents, and parents move toward understanding the individuation process that is occurring. Parents may be more verbal about their feelings than adolescents. Adolescents may not recognize the ambiguity of emotions they are dealing with in this normal process; in fact, they may deny any feelings that do not support their perception of self. This is all part of the struggle for identity. Temperament, environment, understanding of self, and the search for identity impact each person differently.

Erikson identified the adolescent task of social and emotional development as *identity* versus *identity confusion.* If adolescents are not successful in attaining a comfortable level of identity, they will experience identity confusion, unsure of who they are and what they believe. Through the adolescent period, as they struggle with *fidelity* to themselves and others, they struggle with individual identity. Throughout our lives, we may experience times of questioning our identity or reestablishing it, but adolescence is when identity formation is the strongest. Erikson asserted that the strength attained by successful identity is fidelity, and he believed this fidelity becomes evident as a person shows trustworthiness and faithfulness to self, others, and society.

A lack of confirmed identity may result in *defiance.* Defiance may be externalized in behavior, or internalized, creating further confusion for the adolescent, possibly contributing to anxiety, anger, or depression. *Rejection* is the opposite of identity and fidelity. A person whose identity and sense of self are uncertain may have an ideological and unrealistic view of the world and society, placing unrealistically high expectations on self or others. Or, as they reject the views of others, especially families, they may be opinionated and struggle with understanding the perspectives of others.

Erikson affirmed that lasting fidelity cannot exist without trust, and he asserted that established trust has an influence as an individual progresses through future stages. Trust establishes a sense of hope, which leads to autonomy, a sense of independence and will. Autonomy and will lead to a sense of initiative, and after establishing a comfortable sense of initiative, a person is able to move to industry, mastering tasks and achieving a sense of competence. Erikson considered adolescence a life stage that is open for new ideas emotionally and cognitively, as future life plans are a more conscious reality and within tangible reach.

Identity is not established without the influence of environment, family history, and exposure to culture. Social and psychological identities develop out of the gradual integration of all the adolescent has experienced through life, as well as the people they have observed. From infancy, children are conditioned to social participation and they learn about tasks that are dependent on culture. A child has observed role models and varying behaviors and consequences that occur. Adolescents are always questioning, either out loud, or in their minds. Contrast is ever present in our society, causing confusion, even to mature adults. An adolescent needs gradual preparation for life as an adult. Adolescents are fortunate if they have a mentor or positive role model playing an important part in their lives, or positive communication with their family to explore questions and confusion.

Part of the process of identity formation leaves adolescents questioning who they really are. As they sort through family values and expectations, they struggle with weaving their own thoughts to form a unique identity. At the same time, they want to be like their peers. At times, they may feel dominated by peer pressure but not want to conform. This is when a parent can offer the adolescent an out. If adolescents feel picked on by peers because they have a curfew, they can shift the blame to their parents. Most parents will gladly accept responsibility for something like this.

Given the mood changes that accompany adolescent hormones, we may not know what an adolescent's mood will be or when it will shift. Adolescents can seem overly sensitive and shift to anger or sadness, without identifying the reason. They can seem mature and responsible when they need to, but at other times they may revert to silly, childish behavior in the name of fun. My thirteen-year-old daughter had two of her friends sleep over. All was quiet. About one o'clock in the morning, my husband and I were awakened by loud shrieks of laughter and banging. Going downstairs to the kitchen, we found all three girls skating on a pool of water on the kitchen floor and spraying water at each other. Quickly we told them to stop and clean up the mess. I was angry, and I may have added that they were responsible if my kitchen cabinets or floor were ruined. The rest of the night was quiet, and when I awoke in the morning, I could not help but laugh at the memory. It was comical, because when asked what was going on when they were discovered, my daughter responded that she had spilled some water (obviously, more than a little). This is only one example of how adolescents can move quickly in mood and behavior, as well as in their ability to process thoughts. Happily, no one was the worse for wear. The girls bounced back from being yelled at, and the kitchen cabinets and floor were unharmed! Given the variation in moods, it is sometimes hard to know where to meet our adolescents.

Adolescents want to be recognized for who they are—individuals who are not children and not yet adults. They connect dreams, roles, and skills from past to present. As they assert their independence, adolescents will rebel in some form, although with many adolescents it may be less obvious (Erikson 1963). Rebellion in minor ways may prevent a major rebellion later on. Examples of fairly harmless rebellion are talking and dressing differently than adults, having different hairstyles, or having their own norms as a reference for acceptance. Adolescents become defensive if criticized, so save the criticism for more serious situations. Parents and involved adults must speak up if illegal or dangerous activities are happening, or someone is being hurt or demeaned by another person. Aggressive impulses may be intensified during adolescence, and if aggression is unhealthy or unsafe, the adolescent may need guidance in managing these impulses.

Linda E. Powers

Adolescence can be a time of turmoil and chaos for the adolescents as well as their parents. Ambivalence surfaces as adolescents question the values and ideas they were raised with. Their minds go back and forth, trying to find a comfort zone. Some adolescents internalize their turmoil, which could contribute to anxiety and insecurity. Other adolescents may externalize their turmoil with negative or aggressive behavior and attitudes. They may be argumentative, asserting their need for independence and individuality. Hormones are raging, and mood swings are common. Rebellion and defiance may continue at a high level for about two years and then gradually lessen, but it is not uncommon for defiance and rebellion to last for four to six years. Being the parent of adolescents can be challenging as we ride the emotional roller coaster with them. They are feeling just as chaotic as we may feel. Do they know who they really are? They are not sure, but they probably will not admit their uncertainty. They strive to be like their peers yet want to be individuals. Adolescence is also a time of admiring idols and forming ideals, and they may place other people, or ideas on unrealistic pedestals.

Adolescence presents new functions, activities, experiences, and responsibilities. Adolescents, like their younger counterparts, are proud of their accomplishments, but they may also be scared about their future. All new functions require practice and guidance. Like toddlers who are learning to walk, or children who are experiencing anything new, adolescents need adult guidance, although they may not think they do. They gain strength from consistent and wholehearted recognition of their achievements, and these experiences contribute to self-esteem. As they question how to realistically connect roles and skills cultivated earlier in life, they may search for continuity and sameness while simultaneously questioning and searching for the new.

Self-confidence in adolescents can be fragile and varied, depending on what is going on. They may appear self-assured with their demeanor, but inside their minds, they may be questioning their abilities and worth. They may worry quietly and internally how others perceive them. Adolescents are always concerned with who they are and how they meld into a wider circle. Fitting in is important, and much of adolescent behavior reflects the norms of peers. Adolescents are immersed in their peer groups and help each other through discomfort by forming cliques and stereotyping themselves, their ideas, and their enemies. However, they may try different ways to test the ability of their peers' fidelity. Yet, while adolescents are immersed in their peer group, at the same time, each one wants to be an individual. The negative side of peer groups is that they can be clannish and cruel, excluding others whom they consider different. Sometimes, intolerance can be seen as a defense response against identity confusion. As adolescents try to fit into a predominant peer group, they may become more compliant and pleasing to the family or the group, or they may be defiant to the values and beliefs of their family and culture. A young black boy idolizes a superhero, who happens to be white. In his mind, the child may imagine that the admired superhero is black. As he becomes an adolescent and tries to fit into a school culture, which may be predominantly white, he may become more compliant with practices of the culture he is trying to fit in with. He may abandon his earlier thought that the superhero was black, like him, while also rejecting family and culture values. Or he may continue believing that the superhero is black.

Communicating with our adolescents can be a challenge. It is a tricky balance as we try to remember that, while they may physically resemble an adult and show signs of more mature thinking, their minds do not have the logic and formal capacity of a mature adult. Above all, a parent needs to remain a parent, not a best friend. Mutual respect is paramount as parents oversee and guide. Doing activities together builds the relationship. When possible, try to have fun together, whether it is shopping, shooting hoops, or taking a walk.

Formal education does not always provide life skills like money management, schedule planning, organization, and establishing priorities, so adolescents need help to prepare for the responsibilities of adult life. When in conflict with your adolescent, pick your battles. Adolescents need to know where their parents stand on many issues, although they may not agree. They may continually challenge us. During times of disagreement, try compromise and negotiation, placing health and safety as priorities. Learning that people can disagree but find ways to resolve conflict is a valuable life lesson. Adults should avoid judgmental comments, and respect the fact that an adolescent is thinking as an individual.

When your adolescent comes to you with a question

or problem, if you do not know the answer, find resources together. Help your adolescent understand the pros and cons of decisions. Communicate with the "I" message. Instead of saying, "You are such a slob!" try saying something like "I feel frustrated when you do not take your dirty dishes to the kitchen after a snack. I feel that I am not the maid and should not be picking up after everyone all the time." Saying, "You are such a slob" places the adolescent on the defensive, causing retaliation with anger or defiance. When you word the statement in a way that you are assuming some responsibility for how you feel in relation to their actions, you are more likely to get a positive response, even though there will be grumbling.

If your adolescent has made an unkind comment to you, it is okay to say, "It hurts me when you put me down." If an adolescent is misbehaving, it may help to ask yourself, "Why? What could be causing this misbehavior?" If you cannot think of a reason, you can approach your adolescent saying something like, "I feel that something is bothering you." Or, "I do not understand why you are behaving this way", and offer an example. Shouting matches should be avoided, because no one wins. Sometimes an adolescent needs space and time alone, and adults should respect boundaries, yet remain available.

Let adolescents know that feelings are okay; it is how we express those feelings that is either right or wrong. It is okay to apologize to your child or teen if you react impulsively, or with more anger than you intended. An apology helps adolescents realize that negotiation and reconsideration can be options when people disagree or react too intensively.

Remember that much of communication is body language, including tone of voice, posture, and gestures. Ask for adolescents' opinions; they will feel valued. Help them realize that independence is earned. The conflicts we experience with our adolescents are opportunities for growth and learning, for both adolescents and parents. As parents, we can learn more about our adolescent's thoughts. We are still in the position, as parents, to offer guidance—and consequences if necessary. We also may gain insight into the feelings and thoughts they are experiencing but not verbally expressing.

Just as adolescents experiment with ideas and choices, they may experiment with different friendships. You may not feel comfortable with some of the friends, but try to avoid being negative. Instead of trying to forbid the friendship, encourage your teens to invite their friend into your own home, where you have the opportunity to observe. In a kind way, you may point out some of your concerns at a later time.

Parents have the right to authority in their own home, and rules and expectations should be clarified so everyone understands. If expectations are that the family is a team and all members of the team accept responsibility for picking up after themselves, express that expectation. If having a family dinner together is an expectation, work on mutually convenient times.

Today, more than in the past, it is challenging to monitor social media and electronics. Before cell phones, Facebook, and other forms of social media, it was easier for parents to set a limit for no telephone calls after a certain time. Today, we may feel somewhat helpless and overwhelmed with all the sources of technological communication. Adolescents may need to be reminded of the negative effects of sleeping with their cell phones by their pillow. Adolescents should be aware that people have been severely burned by cell phone batteries that have caught on fire spontaneously.

Electronics affect the brain waves and can interfere with good-quality sleep. Being half-alert in order to respond to a text or call from a friend at two o'clock in the morning decreases the quality of sleep for the adolescent. Academic performance and the ability to make good decisions can be affected by poor quality sleep. Many parents restrict all media sources after a certain time, and cell phones are placed in a specified central location in the home.

Parents should avoid power struggles, and they should not let their adolescents walk all over them. If adolescents act impulsively and go against parental suggestions or societal rules, they will learn by having to deal with any consequences. Family meetings are a way to clarify expectations and provide a democratic environment for everyone to offer individual thoughts and feelings. Mutual problem solving can diminish hostility from adolescents and they may not feel overpowered. Sometimes at family meetings, through discussions, a parent may get beyond the surface of a problem, or discover another issue that should be dealt with.

A contract with an adolescent can be as effective as it was with a younger child, with adjustments for age and expectations. Adolescents may appreciate the idea of a contract. Talking with adolescents and asking their thoughts about rewards and consequences offers a more collaborative environment. The adolescents feel involved, and they feel they have some control. Negotiation can be healthy and helpful. Rewards can be phased out as adolescents incorporate their chores and responsibilities into their routine.

Let consequences teach and reinforce responsibility outside the home. If adolescents skip school or do not complete assignments, adults should not cover for them. They need to accept the consequences for their actions. If they are stopped by a police officer for speeding, they need to be responsible for paying the fine. If they do not have the funds to pay the fine, they can reimburse a parent in money they earn or by performing household chores equal to the payment. These experiences provide valuable learning. Adolescents can learn through experience the value of attending team practices or misspending their allowance. Loss of privileges is a good consequence for infringement of the rules or noncompliance. Electronics is a good privilege to remove, and they can have the opportunity to earn the privilege back.

Today, the amount of time a person is exposed to technology is a major concern. As brains are exposed to more and more media and technology, young people risk the ability to adapt to face-to-face communication. Studies have shown that with continuous technology use, the frontal part of brain growth is stunted. Hours and hours spent in front of computer screens, televisions, or blasting music through headphones, affect development of brain circuitry, which is needed to accomplish many milestones.

Excessive use of media can impact adolescents' academic success, abstract thinking, decision-making, empathy, and the ability to develop good communication skills. The stimulation from video games can lead to inattention, distractibility, irritability, increased heart rate, and increased blood pressure, as well as stimulate the body to increase production of stress chemicals.

In addition, exposure to aggressive video games contributes to aggression. Studies suggest that it is the intensity of the violence in the video game, rather than the amount of exposure to violence, that increases aggressive behavior and affects the brain. Because too much technology exposure can impact development of the prefrontal cortex, people who spend too much time in front of technology struggle with understanding the emotions of others, and the result is that they have less empathy. Technology promotes instant gratification, which is not a healthy habit. We need to learn to wait for pleasure, and this comes with further development of the frontal lobe. Prior to cell phones and other technology, people communicated face-to-face, with letters, or talking on the telephone. It is important for adolescents to understand that nonverbal communication gives additional messages. I still find written communication by letter satisfying. The anticipation of something in the mailbox besides bills and advertisements brings a feeling of being appreciated. Someone thought of me enough to take the time to write a letter or address a card. Writing thank-you notes longhand is another way to respectfully communicate.

Since early childhood, adolescents have observed and

lived within a set of moral values. They have picked up on parental, family, and cultural values. The conscience develops, and as they contemplate, adolescents may question and challenge family or parental values, or even the values of society. Lecturing and preaching to adolescents about parental values only widens the gap between the generations. Interestingly enough, young adults who are in their twenties and thirties may return to values similar to those of their parents.

According to the research of Kohlberg and others, adolescents are concerned with maintaining relationships through trust, sharing, and loyalty and they are more likely to take the thoughts and feelings of other people into consideration than younger children. If adolescents move on to the next stage of moral development, they are able to recognize that rules represent agreements about appropriate behavior and are guidelines for society to run smoothly, rather than absolute dictates that must be obeyed because they are the law. In this stage, there is a beginning of recognition of flexibility of rules. It is important to be mindful that moral stages vary among individuals.

As parents and their adolescents continue on their journey together, discipline, in the form of guidance and teaching with unconditional love and respect, strengthens the relationship. In their book *The 5 Love Languages of Children* (2012), Dr. Gary Chapman and Dr. Ross Campbell advise parents to keep their children's emotional tanks filled with love and continue to nurture them. Parents should continue giving the message that they love their child, but they do not condone negative and disrespectful behavior.

By all means, if safety or health is involved, adults must intervene.

While adolescents require less physical attention than younger children, they still need guidance, and they require a lot of emotional energy. Parents should never underestimate their role as parents, and monitoring general health and well being, including sleep, is still within the realm of parental responsibility. Adolescents may need to be reminded that no one is perfect, and no one can do everything; it is okay to rely on others. Parents can help their adolescents identify clear and realistic goals. It is important for parents to accept the fact that adolescents need to establish distance from families, but parents should not doubt their own authority and importance.

Changes in behavior, such as isolating from others, or suddenly becoming more involved with an entirely different group of people, can be red flags. So can a change in sleep or eating habits, excessive rebellion, destructive outbursts, skipping school, or drastic changes in academic performance. A health care professional should be consulted about any concerns, or symptoms of anxiety or depression.

As the individual moves into adolescence and young adulthood, the mode of parenting changes, and as parents we learn to be less vocal, and we temper our advice with appropriate phrases and words. This experience can be challenging, especially as the younger generation adopts lifestyles, beliefs, and language different from those of our generation. We may not understand, but it is important for the relationship to respect the fact that our "child" is now an adult, with the freedom to make individual choices, however different from ours.

When parenting adolescents, remember Erikson's golden rule: Do to another what will advance the others growth even as it advances our own (Erikson 1982, 93).

Chapter 7

*A*dulthood: Continuing
the Journey

The journey continues as we leave adolescence and move into young adulthood, establishing careers and relationships. Reflection on memories, experiences, and relationships, along with new experiences and adventures, offer us the opportunity to learn and grow throughout our adult lives. Increased life span, with improved quality of life, presents us with more opportunities than available to previous generations. Reviewing Erikson's tasks of adult development and incorporating results of new research on aging, we realize we are all part of the circle of life. We observe those around us at various stages, and our understanding of development throughout life helps us appreciate the special qualities in each of us. Experience reminds us of the role that interdependence plays in healthy relationships.

Erikson defined three stages of emotional and social development in adulthood: *young adulthood* with the task of *intimacy* versus *isolation; middle adulthood* with the task of *generativity* versus *stagnation*; and *old age* with the task of *integrity* versus *despair.* Those who develop intimacy in healthy relationships experience the strength of love, enjoying partnership in friendships and romantic relationships. They experience healthy competition and cooperation within groups. Along with intimacy comes a feeling of belonging. A person who has experienced some success in establishing intimacy will feel affiliation with others and more easily see the healthy side of competition, considering it a learning experience with cooperation. There may be times when a person who has attained a level of intimacy feels cut off or isolated. This happens in marriages, romantic relationships, and friendships, as people go through transitions, or struggle to keep up with the responsibilities of daily life. The person who has attained the strengths of hope, fidelity, and love will experience this strength of intimacy again.

Erikson identified isolation as the opposite of intimacy. Those who do not experience intimacy and a sense of belonging within a relationship feel isolated and possibly excluded. They may struggle with working as a member of a team and have difficulty fully cooperating with others to achieve a goal, either in careers or personally. They may lean toward the unhealthy side of competition, seeing it as a battle and a way to win love and support.

Intimacy is not found just in romantic and intimate relationships. The foundation for intimacy begins in infancy as the infant and parent bond. At this time, the relationship is more of a symbiotic nature. As infants grow, they become more independent, learning about give and take in a relationship, but they still need unconditional love, support, guidance, and discipline. Identity is the developmental focus in adolescence, but the foundation of intimacy is strengthened as the adolescent matures and experiences positive and negative aspects in relationships. The adolescent and parent come to know each other well, which is why adolescents can easily push their parents' buttons. Adolescents and parents might relate to each other from opposite poles as adolescents struggle to find identity. While they are struggling from opposite poles, give and take occurs, sometimes not without conflict and anger. As identity strengthens and young adults move into young adulthood, intimacy becomes the main developmental task.

An important aspect of Erikson's theory is that one can go back and revisit previous stages. As mentioned in chapter 1, we revisit identity many times throughout our lives. In young adulthood, the tasks of identity and intimacy may occur simultaneously. Young adults, in their eagerness to form intimacy, may fuse identity with intimacy when they seek a partner. As suggested by some theorists, women may establish intimacy before attaining a sense of identity. As Erikson previously stated, and research has shown, we all go through the developmental tasks, but with individual variations. Erikson, in his book *Childhood and Society* (1963), advised "the strength at any stage is tested by the necessity to transcend it in such a way that the individual can take chances in the next stage with what was the most vulnerable in the previous one." (Erikson 1963, 263). As two people work to build and strengthen a relationship, interdependence strengthens.

Erikson identified the stage of middle adulthood as the time of generativity, when adults have attained a sense of both identity and intimacy. Erikson advised that intimacy and generativity are closely related, but identity and intimacy, with an understanding of culture and society, must be attained first before the task of generativity can be accomplished. Generativity occurs when parents are raising their children, but one does not have to be a parent to successfully accomplish this task. Many adults are generative as mentors, teachers, examples, and models for children, adolescents, and younger adults. With words, through modeling, and drawing on life experiences, this cohort prepares the next generations for the future.

Care is the strength gained from this task, as midlife adults provide care of people, ideas, organizations, and products. This is a time of creativity, procreativity, and productivity. Hope, autonomy, will, initiative, fidelity, and purpose, the strengths arising from childhood and adolescence, are essential for the development of generativity. During this stage, we work together as a team, with a division of labor, as we model responsibility and nurture the next generation. Being a source of guidance for others is energizing and rewarding. Generativity fulfills the human desire to be needed.

The opposite, or negative side of generativity, is stagnation. According to Erikson's theory, those who are not able to care, nurture, and provide guidance for others may be stagnant and unable to attain further development.

Self-absorption or indifference may come with stagnation. Individuals who have not attained a reasonable sense of generativity may experience not only stagnation, but they may feel rejected. They may reject other people and the help others offer. They may feel inferior, isolated, and less autonomous. They may experience problems with trust and hope, which ultimately impacts their ability to feel hopeful and productive. With stagnation, there may be regression to previous developmental tasks, such as intimacy and identity or trust.

Because life takes us along a twisted path, throwing us curves we may not have anticipated, a person may not always feel generative, productive, creative, and able to encourage others. At these times, we may feel temporarily stagnant. Maybe things are not going well, and we feel frustrated and unsuccessful in our generative (parenting) attempts. Maybe there are frustrations with work. We may feel useless and unappreciated. But if we have attained strengths from previous developmental tasks, it is easier to look for the positive and find the occasional golden thread woven among the dull gray threads. Finding one small positive aspect can strengthen us to move ahead.

Generativity, the longest phase of adulthood, can begin as early as the mid-twenties and extend even into the seventies or, in some people who experience good health, the eighties. Entering generativity occurs in some young adults when they first become parents. Others may enter after they have established their careers.

Increased life span, which includes the opportunity for better health and improved quality of life, has given people in this stage an extension to nurture, care, and guide. Moving to the last stage in the life cycle, old age, people meet the task of integrity versus despair. Accomplishing this, they attain the virtue of wisdom.

Many have pointed out that wisdom does not necessarily accompany old age. Development varies among individuals, and life experiences can alter our development, leading some people to develop wisdom before old age. This is affirmed by Mary Catherine Bateson in her book *Composing a Further Life: The Age of Active Wisdom* (2011) and Dr. George Vaillant in his book *Aging Well* (2002).

In her book *Composing a Further Life: The Age of Active Wisdom* (2011), Mary Catherine Bateson, a cultural anthropologist, teacher, and former teaching assistant to Erikson at Harvard, identifies *Adulthood II:* the age of active wisdom. She gives a new perspective on later adulthood, preceding old age, as an opportunity to redefine ourselves, along with redefining our lives, priorities, and passions. It is a time to pursue new adventures or renew past interests. Bateson discusses the challenges (crises/tasks) an individual meets at different developmental stages, reminding that these challenges have the potential to result in either strengths or weaknesses. She revisits Erikson's strengths (virtues) in the life cycle and reaffirms, as Erikson previously stated, that the task of identity is revisited at many stages. She cautions the importance of not limiting the concepts of hope, purpose, wisdom, and other virtues to one specific stage, for hope is renewed and found again at different stages as an individual travels the journey of life. Bateson also observes that people who are less affected by negativity have used adequate coping skills to deal with stress, and they suffer fewer of the negative aspects of aging.

Bateson (2011) identifies that in moving from Adulthood I (Generativity) to Adulthood II, people reflect on what they have done and what they hoped they would accomplish. Adulthood II is when we try new things as we combine our energy and commitment with the wisdom pulled from life experiences. The freedom from the constant responsibilities of child rearing allows time to expand interests and create new goals. In this stage of active wisdom, people have the potential to shape and alter the lives of others, not just in their families but in the public domain as well. People find new avenues to study, learn about, and accomplish. Bateson (2011) compares this stage of life as adding a room to an already existing house, with doorways opening to the other stages in the life cycle. She reminds us that when we add a room to a house, we don't just add a room. That room becomes a part of other rooms in the house and a part of our lives, and we may reorganize to include this new room in our daily living. Compare the life stages to the house. We continue to draw on our experiences, and doorways are openings connecting past with present and eventually future. It is a time to advocate and reflect, speak up, and acquire new skills. Life experiences add to people's confidence, and people are more comfortable advocating and asserting themselves to promote ideas at this stage of life. Comparing life to the house we added a room to, picture a person in the stage of Adulthood II, centered in the house, using experience to advocate for and nurture younger generations.

Erikson (1963; 1982) believed that flexibility remains important throughout the life cycle, as there are always changes to adapt to. One needs to remain flexible and open to life and learning. Identity and intimacy may be redefined in Adulthood II, with the hormonal changes that accompany midlife, and as children leave the nest. Many people revisit spirituality during Adulthood II. For some, it might be exploring new thoughts; for others, it may be returning to a prior religious affiliation. As life continues and retirement approaches, many retirees try new careers or interests, while continuing to offer support and advocacy. Retirement does not mean sitting around being old; it is a new time in life, offering new adventures (Bateson 2011).

Bateson (2011) identifies the developmental crisis of Adulthood II as *engagement* versus *withdrawal,* with the virtue (strength) being active wisdom (2011). She names indifference as the weakness that can occur if a person is not engaged. Bateson also reminds us that people, when talking about events in their lives, identify the events by stages, not necessarily chronological ages. This confirms Erikson's teachings that stages cannot be identified with specific chronological ages, especially in adulthood.

The life cycle continues, and as people move from generativity (Adulthood I) into Adulthood II, they continue guiding, supporting, and creating, weaving past with present, while creating new legacies. Bateson sums it up with the following statement, "We compose our lives in time, improvising and responding to context, yet weaving threads of continuity and connecting the whole as we move back and forth in memory" (Bateson 2011, 181).

Dr. George Vaillant, a principal investigator in the Grant Study, known as the Study of Adult Development at Harvard Medical School, authored three books throughout the study. The seventy-five-year longitudinal study addresses wellness and aging through the decades, with the main goal of identifying predictors of healthy aging. In his book *Aging Well* (2002), Dr. Vaillant states that people who have a positive attitude about life and aging seem to be less affected by the negativity of aging. People with a positive attitude reinvent their lives as they go along, looking for purpose and meaning. A history of warm relationships with family and friends is an important factor, and the openness to continue learning seems to improve interest in life and vitality. Dr. Vaillant's main conclusion (2002) is that experiencing positive, warm relationships has a major effect on positive aging.

Dr. Vaillant used Erikson's model of adult development, writing that the term *developmental tasks* is more appropriate for adult development than stages. He confirms that the development of adults is more fluid and not as sequential as children's developmental stages (Vaillant 2002). Dr. Vaillant has added two additional tasks to Erikson's original description of adult development. He titles the first one, which he added in 1977, *Career Consolidation*, which occurs after intimacy and prior to generativity. Career Consolidation is a time when one is establishing and building a career and attaining mastery of a task that is valuable to both society and self (Vaillant 2002). Dr. Vaillant describes Career Consolidation as a "stage expanding personal identity to assume a social identity within the world of work" (Vaillant 2002, 103). He further states that the contrast to Career Consolidation is *self-absorption*.

Career Consolidation seems to be intermingled with intimacy and generativity, as it involves other people, including family and children. Dr. Vaillant includes parenting as a career, as this task is one where an individual contributes to self and to others. In a review, *Your Life and Your Health*, James Holly, MD, (http://www.setma.com/ Your-Life-Your-Health/pdfs/a-national-health-program.pdf 2014) elaborates on Dr. Vaillant's explanation of parenting as a career. He identifies that being a wife and mother, or husband and father, are tasks that a great amount of energy and time are invested into, for the well being of others and as a value to society (Vaillant 2002). As adults master this task in a career that is valuable to both themselves and society, they move toward generativity.

Dr. Vaillant adds yet another task, entitled *Keeper of the Meaning*, which occurs after generativity (Vaillant 2002). At this time in life, people link the past to the future as they pass traditions on to the next generation, in a social circle wider than parental generativity. The task is to conserve and preserve ideas and products of humankind, institutions, and culture. Dr. Vaillant compares Keeper of the Meaning to a wise judge who offers counsel, and he states that Keeper of the Meaning "involves conservation and preservation of collective products of mankind" (Vaillant 2002, 110). During Keeper of the Meaning, a person's concerns and interests extend beyond one's self and immediate community and show an altruistic approach to promote the most good for the most people. Keeper of the Meaning tasks include using wisdom and justice while passing worthy traditions to the next generations. In his book *Aging Well* (2002), Dr. Vaillant gives Abraham Lincoln as an example, stating President Lincoln "did his utmost to heal and forgive the wounds of the civil war" (p. 46). Bateson's Adulthood II and Vaillant's Keeper of the Meaning are parallel in their tasks and goals.

Dr. Vaillant (2002) identifies *care* as the strength of Keeper of the Meaning, a time when commitment to community, culture and providing guidance to people and organizations, based on experiences, is the common task. Dr. Vaillant (2002) explains that this path leads from the center outward. Grandparents are an example, with grandparents at the center of a circle, relating to all around them. Dr. Vaillant (2002) also affirms Erikson's original life developmental cycle that interest in the middle years expands outward. He states, "The roadmap of development contributes to wholeness and health" (Vaillant 2002, 45).

Interdependence continues to be woven into our lives during middle adulthood. As we follow our own individual path, experience the opportunity to try new things or strengthen existing talents, we guide the younger generations. Through our experience, we teach by example. We provide realistic examples of motivation and caring, which can be inspiring for young people to witness. By remaining active and interesting, we give the message that old age does not have to come prematurely or at a certain time.

Dr. Vaillant (2002) mentions we heal ourselves through the use of healthy coping mechanisms, which are often unconscious. He explains that throughout life, we all use adaptive coping mechanisms, and with maturity, we may use our coping skills more gracefully at seventy than we did at twenty-five. As the frontal lobe of the brain does not reach maturity until sometime in the twenties, or even thirties, our use of healthy coping skills may not surface until that time. Dr. Vaillant cites sublimation and humor as two healthy coping mechanisms. He gives an example of sublimation, using one healthy activity to replace a previous activity. He mentions Winston Churchill, who devoted himself to painting for pleasure after retiring from government service. Humor is another healthy strategy as we turn something negative or unfavorable into humor at ourselves. Humor, as long as it is not derogatory or sarcastic and does not harm self or others, can be a useful way to express one self.

Dr. Vaillant identifies the negative side of Keeper of the Meaning as rigidity (2002). An example of a person who has not accomplished Keeper of the Meaning may be one who shows less interest in passing on traditions and less involvement in promoting the growth and guidance of younger generations. This person may be rigid, self-absorbed, and indifferent.

Mastery of all life tasks is imperfect, because humans are imperfect, and human development is gray, not black and white with clear and precise lines. There are no clear demarcations of each developmental task, for each person develops at an individual rate.

We use our active wisdom, as Keepers of the Meaning, by guiding, teaching, and modeling. We set examples, we mentor, we create, and we encourage not only our own family members but also many members of the younger generations. As life's journey continues, wisdom is accompanied by the ability to connect emotion and thought. With wisdom comes the ability to be a better listener, to hear what others say beyond their words. Perspective is gained, and a person is more aware that there are two sides to everything. My mother had a saying, "There are three sides to every story, your side, the other person's side, and what really happened, which is often somewhere in the middle." As a child and teenager, I tired of hearing that statement. As an adult, I have learned to value her wisdom more with each passing day.

We can all think of examples of people who have aged gracefully, providing a positive example of integrity and wisdom. Several examples of Adulthood II, Keeper of the Meaning, and integrity have passed through my life at different times. A woman who exemplified wisdom, integrity, and Keeper of the Meaning was someone I knew from my childhood into middle adulthood. She was kind but firm in her beliefs about morals and love of family. She served as a solid foundation and graceful example for many people through the years. In my Keeper of the Meaning years, as I was transitioning in my career from a nurse to a therapist, I met another example of Keeper of the Meaning, an elderly woman whose integrity, dignity, courage, and nurturance provided love and support for many, not just members of her immediate family. She was a long-term cancer survivor, a former nurse, a wife, a mother, and a grandmother who remained wise, nonjudgmental, and nurturing to those who crossed her path.

We can all think of personal examples, but some well-known people have offered examples of integrity and dignity as they transitioned through life and adapted in a positive way. When Julie Andrews was no longer able to sing, she transferred her passion to non-singing performances and writing children's books. The books she has coauthored with her daughter provide enchanting stories for children and those who are young at heart. In her recent television series on Netflix, *Julie's Greenroom*, she uses her experiences to offer children information about the arts through puppets. She is a living example of Keeper of the Meaning, engagement, and integrity as she shares her appreciation of people and stories. Mary Tyler Moore is another public example of Keeper of the Meaning and engagement. She was a diabetic who refocused her energy to become a respected and well-known advocate for diabetes treatment and research. Michael J. Fox's promotion for awareness and research of Parkinson's disease shows perseverance and courage while he continues to pursue his career.

It is important to keep in mind that the developmental stage of the parents is as important as the developmental stage of the child. At times, each parent may be in a different developmental stage, depending on circumstances. This can add to the family confusion as each member works through his/her own stage. Grandparents offer a different perspective from their developmental stage. A grandparent who shows wisdom, caring, and love can add a balance to the family dynamic. Grandparents, with their own years of parenting experience, are somewhat removed from the subjectivity and at times can offer objectivity and clear reasoning. They give love and nurturance, enjoying interactions with the grandchildren.

Over the centuries, dating back to the ancient Greeks, there has been ongoing discussion about the balance of emotion and mind, as well as the balance between desire and obedience (Newton 1989). Life can be a constant effort to maintain a balance, to find what Aristotle identified as "the mean between two extremes." We continue to evolve through life's experiences, using our growth to guide others, and at the same time we create new meaning in our lives. Conclusions from the Harvard Study (2002), Bateson's (2011) research, and the research of others, show the importance of finding a balance between work and play. Creativity fosters vitality, enthusiasm, and energy, often contributing to elderly people appearing younger than their stated chronological age. As adults, our "play" time is often creating and following new ideas, our own as well as those of others. Play and recreation are essential for adults in maintaining a balance and managing stress. Studies have suggested that those who found it easier to play in childhood found it easier to incorporate play into adult midlife.

Generativity, Keeper of the Meaning, and engagement evolve into active wisdom. In the beginning of his book *Aging Well* (2002), Dr. Vaillant quotes Socrates, "I enjoy talking with very old people. They have gone before us on a road by which we, too, may have to travel, and I think we do well to learn from them what it is like" (Vaillant 2002, 57). Following this quotation, Dr. Vaillant discusses longevity as both a blessing and a curse. Medical science has given us tools for healthier living. Almost daily we hear stories of elderly people experiencing life. Sometimes those stories reflect energetic, vital, and healthy elders. Some elders, despite illness or difficult times, retain faith and optimism. Other times, the stories tell of sadness and despair, or neglect and abuse of the older generation. Sometimes disease or poor health hastens the aging process. Why are some people more energetic than others? Why do some people seem to age quickly, while others remain vital beyond their years?

Often the older generation is associated with decline, loneliness, and death. We associate zest and success with the young. Research shows youth are not the only ones with success and vitality. As we learn to adapt to changes, such as decreased energy level, inability to run as fast as we once could, and diminished hearing, we find ways to compensate. We may take more time to appreciate life. With age, tolerance and patience often improve. As grandparents, we may be more tolerant of some of our grandchildren's behaviors than we were of our children's. We may show more patience in dealing with others. We have learned many of life's lessons, leading to wisdom. Wisdom, in turn, contributes to a sense of integrity, which has been described as the evidence of grace and satisfaction with self and life in the later years. Integrity has also been described as a spiritual sense of acceptance and dignity, in spite of bodily decline.

Many physical, emotional, and cognitive changes occur naturally with the aging process. Nerve conduction slows, reflexes are not as quick, and eyesight diminishes, as does hearing. Memory, especially short-term memory, may not be as sharp. As the baby boomer cohort advances in age, we are hearing more and more about ways to preserve the body and mind. Hints for healthy aging are everywhere.

Erikson identified the negative aspect of old age as despair. How easy would it be to let the declining changes that accompany aging and disease take over our existence, especially in our current world that places an emphasis on youth and perfection? Research from observations and studies like Bateson's (2011) and the Harvard Study (2002) shows that in the face of adversity and aging, life continues to have meaning, and the wisdom gained from experience helps future generations evolve. As elderly people view their lives, and contemplate the paths they took, appreciating their blessings and remembering the positive, they attain integrity, which leads to acceptance and peace. If they regret their life, lament their choices, and dwell on the negative, they will be in a state of despair and grief.

Dr. Vaillant, in *Aging Well* (2002, 54), reminds that Erikson suggests that one of the life tasks of integrity is for the old to show the young how not to fear death. Dr. Vaillant (2002) quotes Henri Amiel, who in 1874 stated, "To know how to grow old is the master-work of wisdom, and one of the most difficult chapters in the great art of living" (Vaillant 2002, 54). It is important to ask older people about their life journeys and the things that made a difference in their lives. What have these wise elders done? How have they faced adversity in their lives? What do they hope to pass on to future generations?

As we travel life's journey, we have a better understanding of life and of people if we understand the basics of life development. Understanding the stages of life gives us more tolerance of the developmental tasks and challenges others are faced with at their particular developmental stage. The stage of emotional development of a parent interacts with the child's developmental stage. In the next chapter, we will explore variations of parental development with the developmental stages of childhood.

Erikson's Stages of Adulthood Development Revised with the Works of Mary Catherine Bateson and Dr. George Vaillant

Stage	Task	Strength
Young Adulthood	Intimacy versus Isolation	Love
Young-Middle Adulthood	Career Consolidation versus Self-Absorption	Care
Middle Adulthood	Generativity versus Stagnation	Care
Adulthood II	Engagement versus Withdrawal/ Indifference	Active Wisdom
Keeper of the Meaning	Care versus Rigidity	Care
Old Age	Integrity versus Despair	Wisdom

(Bateson 2011; Erikson 1982; Vaillant 2002)

Chapter 8

*A*dapting

We are continually adapting to change. Sometimes it feels like as soon as we become used to something, another change occurs. Changes in our own process can lead to new awareness and new experiences. Other people evolve, and this, in turn, may impact our relationship with them. The universe is always changing our environment, whether it is our family, social environment, changes in the world, cultural adaptations, or weather variations. Rapidly changing thoughts and actions of each generation influence everyone. The journey of life is never stagnant, although sometimes it seems that way when we feel stuck in a not so comfortable situation. As parents, it may feel like we do double or triple duty as we adapt to the growth and development of our children. Simultaneously, we continue to grow and develop ourselves. Understanding these developmental changes aids us in strengthening all of our relationships.

Past influences affect a person's attitudes and behavior,

which is why behavior can sometimes be puzzling. People who had a traumatic experience in childhood or adolescence might experience anxiety or fear in response to events that remind them of that time. Trauma is not just related to horrific situations like war exposure or a major accident. Trauma comes in many forms, from the slightest degree to a serious, life-impacting event. Witnessing a bad accident, experiencing the death of a family member, or a profoundly negative social interaction, can influence attitudes and behavior, especially when people are reminded of the trauma. Because people vary in their responses to situations and their coping skills, trauma affects people in different ways. A situation that might be traumatic for one person may not create as much of a problem for another person. We have more tolerance when we understand the normal developmental process, acknowledging that the norm can vary according to an individual, the environment, and an individual's response to events. Understanding the behaviors that may accompany the developmental stage is key to maintaining successful relationships.

Erikson affirmed, and Dr. Vaillant (2002) and others have agreed, that a person can't reach the stage of generativity until successfully accomplishing the tasks of identity and intimacy. Sometimes people are parents before they have established intimacy. There is no right or wrong. As the saying goes, "It is what it is." That goes for developmental stages as well. We cannot hurry our development along; nor can we pause it. It happens as it is meant to. Developmental milestones, whether in childhood or adulthood, can't be forced, rushed, or slowed down, but they can be encouraged. They cannot be manipulated, controlled, or willfully adjusted. Developmental milestones evolve, and the best way to handle relationships in a positive way is to understand these stages.

People who experienced difficulty establishing intimacy or positive relationships might show behaviors indicating exclusivity. They may have a fear of commitment and closeness and keep to themselves, not getting involved in any emotionally intimate relationship. They may appear to be uninterested in others or picky about associations with other people, but deep down, they may want warm and close relationships. People who experienced difficulty with the stage of generativity in middle adulthood might appear to be rejecting or uncaring, showing little obvious concern for the well being of others. Hidden but caring feelings are kept behind an emotional wall. People who did not achieve a sense of industry in childhood may show inertia and lack of motivation.

The developmental stage of the parent plays as important a part in the interactions between child and parent as does the developmental stage of the child. For example, if a fifteen-year-old becomes a parent, she is still struggling with identity, the developmental task of adolescence. She does not have a strong sense of identity and self-understanding. Her identity has not had the time or the experiences to strengthen. She is limited in her experience of intimacy. Although she may have felt a sense of intimacy with a parent or sibling or friend, she is not developmentally ready to meet the task of young adulthood, which is intimacy. The physical/sexual intimacy she experienced with the father of her child is not the same as the intimacy experienced between two mature adults who have each reached a sense of individual identity and may be ready for a mature, intimate, long-term relationship. While she may be lacking in identity strength and mature intimacy experience, she will begin the caregiving associated with the task of generativity. The same is true of an adolescent boy who becomes a father. If he is involved in the child's life, he enters generativity before he has accomplished the strengths of identity and intimacy. This is not saying the fifteen-year-old will not be a good parent.

Perhaps the adolescent female will accomplish her task of identity while invested in parenthood. Intimacy may come at a later time, when she is ready as an individual to commit to a long-term relationship. Her career may develop while she is involved in the career of parenting. When her child is a teen, the parent, who became a parent as a teen, may feel more understanding toward her child, as her teen years were not that long ago. Or, she may feel envious that her child, or her other friends as teens, are experiencing the fun and freedom that she missed.

Love is the most important ingredient for a successful parent-child relationship. With love comes nurturing. Parents and caring adults in the life of the teen parent are important in providing a supportive environment. As a teen parent receives nurturing, she will find it easier to provide the love and nurturing her child needs. As she receives loving support from family or other resources, the adolescent will continue to develop.

A woman who gives birth to her third child at the age

of thirty-six is in a different stage of development than the teen mom. She is in generativity, already experienced in caregiving. She has most likely established a sense of identity and intimacy, although she will revisit identity many times in the future as life evolves. The same holds true for a dad's developmental process. Parents must adapt to the developmental stages of all their children, meeting each one at their level. Challenging? Yes! Adapting will differ, depending on what stage of development each child is at. It will be different for the third time parent whose older children are in toddlerhood or preschool than if they are in latency.

What about the parent who has another child when her two older children are adolescents, or one an adolescent and one at latency age? Developmental stages will differ, and the challenge of adapting to multiple developmental stages within the family dynamic falls to the parents/caregivers. The parenting journey may begin when one or both parents are in Career Consolidation. Career Consolidation may continue as part of individual identity as parents move to generativity. At the same time, tasks and dynamics of intimacy may change as the parents prepare for and adjust to parenthood.

Someone who becomes a first-time parent around the age of forty may have experienced a longer stage of intimacy, and her identity as an individual may be stronger. She may have attained Career Consolidation, but as a new mom, she revisits identity. She may have successfully reached Career Consolidation with many years of experience, or she may be in the midst of Career Consolidation. Tasks of development will vary according to life's circumstances. There is no rigid timetable for the developmental tasks, especially the tasks of adulthood. Flexibility is key.

A grandparent who has raised children, and is in what Mary Catherine Bateson (2011) identifies as Adulthood II, may find herself as a surrogate parent for her grandchildren. She has completed generativity and for whatever reason now is assuming full-time care for her grandchildren. She must adapt to whatever developmental stage each grandchild is in. Perhaps her wisdom, gained from past experiences, gives her more insight or tolerance, although her physical energy may not be what it was twenty years earlier. With each relationship, a person brings personal characteristics and strength. Older adults learn to adapt when physical limitations restrict physical activity. With flexibility of mind, we can continue to enjoy togetherness with youth.

Changes in the environment or a change in family dynamics can impact the developmental stages, both in children and adults. As mentioned earlier, all of us, children and adults alike, may regress when fatigued, or during times of transition or stress. This regression may be mild and unnoticeable to others. It may be as simple as choosing a comforting and favorite activity to reduce stress or to rest after a long day. For an adult or child, regression may show in leaning toward comfort foods. Transitions, like a new school, a new home, the beginning of the school year, or an introduction to a new activity or person, can lead to slight regression through the adjustment period. Major events like a death in the family, parental divorce, the deployment of a parent who is in the military, or serious illness impact development.

A person may or may not show noticeable regression. Just as development among individuals varies, the way a person displays anxiety, depression, or stress, with resulting regression, will differ. A child who was toilet-trained may start having accidents. Language development might stall. A child who previously fell asleep easily may become anxious at bedtime. A child may become more attached to a parent or caregiver or be hesitant to adapt to a change in routine or participate in a new experience. A child may internalize his anxiety and frustration, and these feelings emerge in behaviors like tantrums and emotional reactions that are exaggerated in accordance with the degree of the event. Adults also may internalize their anxiety or frustration, resulting in behavior and attitude changes. Anxiety may be masked by withdrawal, over involvement to avoid ritualistic behaviors, or other symptoms.

Depression does not always show itself with sadness. Like anxiety, it can be masked with anger, withdrawal, aggression, or other behavior changes. Children can't always verbalize their emotions, but they observe more than we may realize. Memories might exist from events that occurred when a child was very young and preverbal. These memories may not be conscious, or expressible, or identifiable, but they are there and can affect a person's response.

Grief does not only come with the death of a loved one. Grief can come to any of us, at any time, with a loss, major change, or threat to normal life functioning. Grief is an individual process; each person experiences it differently, for different reasons and with different intensities. The death of a pet, or a family member, or death of a friend will elicit the grieving process. Being diagnosed with a serious, possibly terminal illness, or having a loved one diagnosed with a serious illness, can cause grief. The loss of a job, relationship, or home will cause grief. Retirement is a major transition, and some people go through the grieving process at this time; they may wonder about their purpose in life since they previously identified with their job. The aging process can create a feeling of grief as a person's awareness focuses on any decline in functioning, no matter how slight.

Many have heard and read about the five stages of grief that Dr. Elisabeth Kubler-Ross identified in the 1960s. As she studied people who were terminally ill, Dr. Kubler-Ross observed certain stages that happened with the process. As time passed, it became obvious that these stages of grief occurred not only in a terminally ill person but also in a person who lost a loved one to death. Further observation and studies have shown that grief is not only associated with death or terminal illness. Today, we understand that grief can occur with any loss. Divorce is a trigger of grief, as it presents major life changes to all parties involved. Grief is a response to a loss—a loss of lifestyle, a person, a job, a friend, a home, or even a loss or change of status we have identified with. Grief differs among individuals in severity, timing, and responses. There is no right or wrong way to grieve. Grief is not like ascending or descending a set of stairs. People cannot be rushed through the grieving process. There is no timetable.

The first stage of grief is denial, when a person partially or completely denies the existence of a problem, a loss, or a diagnosis. In this initial stage, a person may appear to not comprehend the seriousness, or even the existence of grief, denial, or the problem itself. Denial, a defense mechanism, unconsciously protects us until we become used to the information that something in our lives will change.

Grief can come unexpectedly, shocking us. Many people do not realize they are in denial, and even those of us who are fully aware of the process may be caught off guard and not realize the full extent of our denial until later. I experienced this when I received a diagnosis of lymphoma in December 2013. My symptoms had mimicked asthma symptoms, which had been my companion for years. Although I was unusually tired, I brushed off thoughts of a serious illness, thinking an increased cough and shortness of breath with exercise caused my symptoms. Even when I was given the information of possible lymphoma, I remained in partial denial until the biopsy results. Even awareness and understanding of the process do not give us immunity to the stages of grief. We can't avoid grief.

As the grief process continues, a person moves to the second stage, anger, which can manifest in many ways. A person may seem to be constantly angry, about everything, and the slightest provocation can lead to increased anger. A person may project anger onto other people or things, including medical professionals. Some people express anger toward God as they struggle to understand why this is happening. It is not uncommon for people to express anger to the people they feel safest with, family and close friends.

Some people may internalize their anger and withdraw or isolate. People vary in the way they express their anger during the grieving process, and an expression of anger with grief may be different from the person's usual way of expressing anger.

The third stage, bargaining, follows anger. People may find themselves making bargains or promises. Bargaining may be done with God. Or a person might think, *If only I had done this or that, this would not have happened.* Children might wonder (and not verbally express) if, had they done something differently, the event would not have happened. For example, *If I had gotten better grades, maybe my parents would not have divorced. If I had behaved better, maybe … would not have happened.* Even though no one is at fault, children may assume responsibility, and they often will not verbalize it. This can lead to guilt. Reassurance, validation, and acceptance are crucial throughout the grieving process but especially during the bargaining stage, because this is when a person's self-worth may be low.

The fourth stage of grief, depression, can show its face in many ways and many depths. Depression can be shown with sadness and less interest in the usual things. Depression can cause changes in sleeping and eating patterns. Symptoms may include complete or partial isolation and avoidance; a person may appear uninterested and aloof. Or symptoms can move to the other end of the spectrum with complete withdrawal or inability to function. Behavior may change and become reckless compared to the person's norm, a way of unconsciously fighting the depression, but not a healthy way to overcome it. There may be sadness over loss, poor health, or a change in a person's independence.

The final stage, acceptance, occurs when people rebuild their lives. The change or loss will remain a memory, but people can move on and function in life. Like Erikson's stages of social and emotional development, the grieving stages are flexible, and a person may move back and forth between the stages. Anger and depression are two stages commonly revisited as a memory is triggered or something reminds us of the past, whether it is a person or an event. Life continues, and we move on, but the loss is not forgotten. The intensity of sadness or anger may resurface at predictable times, like around holidays or a birthday. At other times, a song, a story, or an event that triggers a memory may stir emotions.

Grief is no longer a quiet, hidden experience. Attitudes and knowledge about grief are much healthier than years ago. In the past, people avoided discussing the topic of grief. It can be frustrating and lonely to not have grief acknowledged. I experienced this when my second pregnancy ended at nineteen weeks. At that time (1976), the loss of an unborn infant was often not acknowledged with a memorial service unless the infant was born at full term or nearly full term. I could feel people were avoiding the topic as I searched for reasons for the loss and looked for ways to attribute the loss. After several weeks, blood tests revealed that I had an Epstein-Barr virus, which had caused minor symptoms for me but could have affected the health of my unborn son, resulting in loss. Knowing a possible cause for the loss of our child eventually helped.

Today, a support group called SHARE (www.share.org) is available for parents who lose an infant from any time after conception to three months after birth. Today, grief is openly acknowledged, and parents can have a memorial service or any other remembrance they wish. I have often wished that this opportunity had been available to us at that time, to help bring closure and acknowledge that this fetus, although he never lived, was our child and family member.

There is a black-and-white portrait painted by Thomas Attig in the late 1800s or early 1900s that clearly shows how people did not express or share their feelings of grief. In this portrait, several people are sitting in a room, obviously mourning the loss of a loved one. Faces are either expressionless or absent, portraying lack of emotion. There is no eye contact, and people are not even looking at each other. Some people face in opposite directions, a clear message of avoidance. Society has a much healthier attitude about grief today, as we realize a loss has occurred, and part of the process of acceptance of the loss is acknowledgment and validation.

Everyone hopes for a healthy child who will have a carefree life. We never want our children to be hurting physically or emotionally, and we want their lives to be without struggle. But, as life has it, children may be born with anomalies, or during childhood they may develop a serious or terminal illness or suffer an injury that might impair their functioning. In these cases, development may not progress as it would in a child not afflicted with congenital anomalies, illness, or injury. There may be a slower progression, or growth may be stunted socially, emotionally, or cognitively. The important key is to meet these children at the developmental stages they are at and to help them progress to an individual potential. Consulting a health care provider for possible referrals for support and further information is beneficial.

For example, a child with cerebral palsy may have physical, cognitive, and emotional deficits to varying degrees. Social and physical development may not progress at the normal rate. Children who are diagnosed as being on the autism spectrum may have varying intellectual levels, and language development may differ, along with varying social and emotional development. Children with cystic fibrosis, muscular dystrophy, and other diseases will vary in development. Meet each individual child where he/she is.

When a child is born with deficits, is ill, injured, faces a serious surgery or treatment, parents may go through the grieving process. This is an unexpected loss. Depending on a person's coping skills and the nature of the situation, grieving may be slight and not impact normal functioning and health, or it may be deeper. Parents should not hesitate to reach out for support at these times. The loss of a healthy child impacts the lives of all family members in many ways. A parent questions, "Why me? Why my child?" Intimacy in relationships may be affected. Parents may revisit identity as they try to readjust and fit all the pieces of their life together with this unexpected change. Identity and career may be re-explored, along with questions about the purpose of life. Hope may diminish. Anger may surface, or symptoms of depression may arise. Sometimes parents return from a downtrodden state with new energy, a new cause to advocate for, and a renewed dedication. When this happens, a sense of initiative and industry may resurface. There is no timetable for this process, because it is individual. Seek professional help and search for resources. Your pediatrician or family physician is a good place to start.

Many of us have had the experience of parenting our parents as they became older and less independent. It may or may not have been a gradual onset. Throughout our lives, our parents nurtured us, and we looked to them for support and instructions. Our parents were role models for us. Suddenly, we are providing physical or emotional care, managing their finances, or functioning as advocates for their health care. To me, it felt uncomfortable to be making decisions that impacted my mom's life, decisions that she always made for herself. Role reversal. I was the parent, and she was the child. Where did my mom go?

As my mom's dementia progressed, I recognized I was in denial, and I knew denial was part of my grieving process. She thought her relatives who had passed were still alive. She would ask me, "Have you heard from Grammie and Grampa today?" Or she thought she needed to visit her parents or siblings who had passed. When I gently reminded her they were no longer with us, she would ask, "When did that happen?" I would tell her the time of their passing and associate it with another event she could recognize. Then she would remember. Many times, we visited the cemetery, and she expressed awareness of family members' passing. A while later, she would forget again. One day, as I was driving her to a doctor's appointment, she said to me, "Does Mother know I am with you?" Bang! Reality hit, and I came out of my denial. I was grieving for the parent who had always been my supporter and who had given me strength. It was time for me to move on.

When I visited my mom in assisted living, she kept asking to go home. She wanted to live with me, and this could not happen. She took care of her mother in the family home, and my grandmother took care of her mother in the family home. I was the generation that broke the tradition, and I experienced guilt. My mom never said anything to cause my guilt, but I felt it.

It was my responsibility to advocate for her and make her remaining time with us as good as possible. I was an only child; thus, everything fell on me. I was her advocate for finances, medical decisions, and decisions about living. I had no siblings to talk things over with. Many times, I felt alone and overwhelmed. I had the support of my family and friends, without which I could not have made it through. However, I was still alone, parenting my parent at the end of her life. I experienced the grieving process before she passed, as I was slowly losing her as the parent I had always known. While parenting my mom was difficult, these experiences made me stronger. I felt pulled in many different directions, questioning and sometimes not finding answers. In hindsight, my years of professional experience and education were a blessing. I could recognize the stages I was going through, and I knew in time the process would evolve. I needed patience.

However, due to circumstances, some parents are not able to provide unconditional love and nurturing. Unfortunately, some people did not have a parent as a strong role model. At these times, a child, often the oldest, may take on responsibility, often assuming responsibility for younger siblings. This child is referred to as a parentified child, as she takes on the role of a parent while still a child. People who have not had parents as strong role models will grieve a parent in a different way; they may grieve not having had a parent during part, or all, of their childhood.

Our parents were our role models and growing up we critiqued them. If we noticed traits in our parents that we did not like, we may have criticized them. Adolescents normally go through a period when they think their parents are stupid and annoying, and as teens, we may have felt embarrassed by our parents. Annoyances may pass with adolescence, but sometimes they remain. However, we have the option to change. For example, if someone's parent or grandparent was a constant whiner or complainer, the adult child has the option to avoid becoming a whiner or complainer, and may look for different ways to express frustrations. If a parent is punitive, abusive, emotionally unavailable, or overly critical, the adult child has the opportunity to learn from the experience and develop a healthier relationship with his/her own children. Some people may have thought their parents were too strict, and these people have the option to reexamine discipline and change the way they parent their own children.

Yes, we parent our parents, and we parent other people as we nurture and provide care, guidance, love, support, and encouragement. We may experience this at different stages during our adult development. When I experienced parenting my parent, I had been in the stage of generativity for some time. My daughters were grown. I was in Bateson's (2011) Adulthood II and Dr. Vaillant's (2002) Keeper of the Meaning. I was also experiencing personal and career changes. Professionally, I was a pediatric nurse and a triage nurse. I had recently earned a master's degree in counseling psychology, and I was starting a new career as a therapist. I was in Dr. Vaillant's Career Consolidation (2002) yet again as I began my new career.

Life continues, despite overwhelming responsibilities and frustrations. Eventually, things work out, and life is good again. Then there is another twist in the road to test our strength. We develop coping mechanisms. Some of these skills are healthy, like Dr. Vaillant's example of Winston Churchill converting his passion for politics and government to painting (2002). A healthy sense of humor can help us get through difficult situations, as long as no one is hurt or discriminated against. Some coping skills are unhealthy. There are many self-help books, therapists, and support groups that offer education, encouragement, and support. Chapter 10 will suggest strategies that have worked for many people. Different strategies may work for different people, but in the end, it is helpful for all of us to understand the developmental process of life.

Chapter 9

Relationships

The word *relationship* is defined as a connection of two or more people, concepts, or objects (*Merriam-Webster Dictionary* 2017). Throughout our lives, we are involved in multiple relationships, beginning with our connections with our family of origin.

There are different types of interpersonal relationships, varying in degrees of intensity. Intimate and long-term relationships, such as those with family and close friends, require mutual energy and respect. Relationships with friends, acquaintances, and coworkers are less intense but still require respect and energy if they are to remain positive. Healthy relationships are interdependent, providing a give and take quality, with each person having self-awareness as an individual, yet simultaneously involved in the give and take between persons.

The amount of give and take within a relationship can change, depending on circumstances. For example, infants are dependent on a parent or caretaker for all their needs, but as they develop and gain more independence, the give and take changes. As they individuate, reaching adulthood, they are self-reliant and enter into healthy, interdependent relationships. In a marriage or partnership, the needs change throughout the relationship, depending on life circumstances. For example, if one partner or spouse is ill, the ill partner or spouse may temporarily rely more on the other partner than when they are both in good health. At other times, one of the partners or spouses might require extra emotional support because of job stress or extended family stress. A friendship might flourish when two people enjoy the time spent together, yet each person maintains a sense of self-awareness. In this friendship, each person might rely on the other person at different times for a particular need. Understanding where other people are in their lives is the hallmark of connecting in a meaningful relationship. In a successful and healthy relationship, a person can accept and try to understand the other person's developmental stage, as well as the person's needs and virtues.

Codependent relationships are considered unhealthy. In a codependent relationship, one person may enable another person's unhealthy behavior and thoughts. The give and take is not equal. In a codependent relationship, one person relies too much on the other person, and there is not interdependence or mutual exchange. Often, one person attempts to control another, resulting in the other person not being able to fulfill individual potential. One person in a codependent relationship may rely too heavily on the partner to meet individual needs. Another example is when a person depends on another person to meet all needs in order to feel happy. Overly reliant people do not rely on themselves to seek their own path. One participant in a relationship may have an excessive and unhealthy tendency to take on responsibility for another person as a means to boost self-esteem through self-sacrifice. It is important for each person in a relationship to maintain individuality. With healthy interdependence, each person in the relationship maintains individuality and is respectful of the other person's individual potential. The participants work together, allowing relationships to prosper.

The world is filled with natural energy, and this natural energy is what we draw from to maintain our own healthy energy. We need a healthy balance of energy and power in relationships. Threatening or intimidating another person is not acceptable in a relationship, although it happens far too often. The power and control that go on in a relationship are often unconscious. Violence often comes from a need to dominate or control, and as this continues, the weaker person feels as if personal energy is depleted. As the controlling person seeks power and energy, the controller feels stronger. As people compete for energy, power, and control, the equilibrium needed in a healthy relationship is lost. Energy gained in this way does not last long and is not real. This lack of respect and imbalance of power in a relationship is not healthy.

Gaining power or attention, by whatever means, will temporarily satisfy the need to be powerful and controlling. This need may come from an underlying feeling of insecurity, and gaining power helps this person feel important and strong. James Redfield, a former therapist who worked with troubled teens, authored the best-selling fictional book *The Celestine Prophecy* (1993) and subsequent books in the series. He gives names and examples of four types of unhealthy power relationships. He refers to these as "control dramas," and he offers that these dramas often begin in the family of origin as family members seek power and control. He names the four dramas: intimidator, interrogator, aloof, and poor me.

Redfield states, "Irrational power struggles always occur when we find ourselves losing energy because of someone's manipulations of our attention, and we fight back to control the situation" (*Celestine Prophecy: An Experiential Guide* 1995, 90). Redfield identifies the *intimidator* as a person who demands attention through force, loudness, anger, and threats, which can be physical, emotional, or verbal. This attitude creates anxiety. If a parent displays these patterns, children and others feel weak and powerless in response. Recipients of the intimidator's power and control may adopt the poor-me defense. They feel energy is taken from them, and they believe they are weak and have no power. In response, they may use their victimized feeling as a way to face life.

Redfield names the second power force as the *interrogator*, a person who controls not by physical force or obvious control, but by continually criticizing and questioning everything someone says and does. Constantly questioning and criticizing, without offering praise or encouragement, the interrogator does not know how to validate or communicate in a positive manner. An interrogator does not listen and validate, but seems to have all the answers for other people. The interrogator watches everything in the environment, taking energy from others with hostile and critical comments. Children and others may respond by adopting either the poor-me drama or the drama of being aloof. Aloofness is displayed with a detached or mysterious attitude, as people struggle with their own fears and unresolved worries. Detachment is their defense to protect themselves from getting too close to others, or having to deal with being observed and criticized.

These patterns, established in childhood, create unhealthy energy in relationships. In these scenarios, energy is drained from everyone. Abuse of all kinds emerges where there is an imbalance of power, sometimes leading to violence (Redfield 1993). Various people have described abuse and power in different ways. The sad fact is that these situations often occur below the level of consciousness, and the behavior becomes habitual. Redfield's examples provide one scenario of the abuse that occurs in relationships having an imbalance of power. Whether we reference Redfield's explanation or another one, these power relationships are prevalent and contribute to the development of unhealthy emotions.

Communication is necessary to maintain any relationship, and respect is a key factor in good communication. It is important to show respect to other people, even if their opinions differ from our own. The word *communication* is derived from the Latin word *communiare*, which means to share (*Merriam-Webster Dictionary* 2017). When we communicate, we share information, providing a means of connection. As we share with words, we also share with nonverbal language. A person's stance, posture, facial expressions, and tone of voice play a major role in communication. If people have their arms crossed in front of them, do not make eye contact, and slightly turn their head away, they give the message that they are closed and not open. The nonverbal message conveyed may be annoyance, anger, or detachment. When people make eye contact, listen, and are physically in more relaxed positions, they seem more approachable.

In good communication, it is important to have congruence between verbal and nonverbal messages. Congruence, meaning harmony, compatibility, or consistency, reflects genuine and honest communication and does not leave doubt or confusion about the message. For example, if I come home and in a sarcastic voice and with a look of negativity on my face say, "I had a great day," my verbal and nonverbal messages are inconsistent. What do I really mean? My verbal message literally says I had a good day. My nonverbal messages say otherwise. If someone says to me, "Are you angry?" and I have the stance and facial expression of someone who is frustrated and angry, but verbally I say, "No, I am not angry," the message is confusing. The written content of email does not reflect the full meaning, and any message that would have been conveyed by tone of voice or body language is lost. Any message of importance, or one bearing emotion, should not be communicated in email, texting, or similar forms of technological communication. When I was working full-time as a therapist, I had a poster in my office that read,

"Someone may not believe what you say, but they will believe what you do." This poster prompted many discussions with children, teens, and families.

Listening is an act of love and is a key factor in communication, showing respect. Validation is also important. Validating is not agreeing with, but acknowledging that we have heard the other person. We may not agree with what another person is saying, but we can acknowledge that we have heard: "I may not agree with you, but I heard you." Reflecting, or stating back what you heard, is helpful in communicating to your child that you heard what was said. Validating is important in disciplining children. As we guide and teach others the lessons we want them to learn, their feelings and thoughts need to be acknowledged.

Just as we need to take responsibility for our actions, we need to be responsible in our communication. We accept responsibility for ourselves and our feelings when we use statements that reflect what we are thinking or doing, as opposed to statements that are accusing or interrogating. A parent may say to a child, "I would like you to pick up your dirty clothes and put them in the hamper. I feel frustrated when I see all your dirty clothes lying around." With this statement, the parent is acknowledging her own frustration and is clearly requesting what needs to be done. If a parent makes an accusatory statement, and does not use an "I" statement, a child may react defensively. If a child hears accusatory and negative comments often, the child may begin to feel negative and inferior. An accusatory tone and constant interrogations can lead to defensiveness and anger in the other person. The 'I' statements may feel awkward at first, but they demonstrate that we accept responsibility for our thoughts, feelings, and actions. When a person decides to use more 'I' statements, I recommend they start with less important things rather than a major issue. If a child hears parents accept responsibility for their own feelings, the child is more likely to come around and be a team player. The parent has shown by example. When positive communication occurs, respect is more likely to become a habit. Parents are the facilitators in communication, and set the tone and the patterns. These guidelines for communication apply to all relationships.

Boundaries are important in any relationship. Boundaries include respecting other people and their privacy. Compliance with appropriate boundaries also means understanding the developmental level of the other person, as well as any circumstances impacting the person at that time. When a person is emotionally enmeshed with another person and boundaries are lacking, each person loses individuality. This applies to all relationships, whether the relationship is between two adults, adults and children, groups of children, or professionals.

As we think of a child as a whole or unified individual, it helps to keep in mind that many parts are developing simultaneously, each at its own rate. Physical, emotional, social, speech/language, cognitive, spiritual, sexual, and ethical development integrate through the overall developmental process, forming an individual. Just as social and emotional development begins in the family environment, ethical development and spiritual development originate there as well. Children, as early as infancy, pick up on vibes in the environment, even if a word is not spoken. They learn by observation and absorption. If a child witnesses an adult showing prejudice, even subtle prejudice through facial expressions or actions, that child may adopt a biased attitude. If a child is in an environment that accepts diversity and demonstrates respect for others with words and actions, this trait will most likely be ingrained in the child. Children observe and learn from their parents' and grandparents' spiritual beliefs. If children have had a foundation for their spiritual development, they are able to make their individual choices later, after weighing facts and thoughts.

Communication is about connecting, and discipline is more effective when we are connected with our children. Discipline with adequate communication can be a learning experience. Discipline, which is teaching and guiding, should be based on nurturing the whole child. We can ask ourselves, "What lesson do we want our child to learn? What is the best way I can help them understand? Why are they acting this way? What is the best way to redirect them? Is there a way I can help them reframe their thoughts?"

In their books *No Drama Discipline* (2014) and *The Whole Brain Child* (2011), Dr. Daniel Siegel and Dr. Tina Payne-Bryson address ways to discipline a child and at the same time help the child learn to associate behaviors with consequences. They affirm that the brain is a social organ, always open to learning, especially social learning. The two sides of the brain have different functions, which can be opposing. One part of the brain deals with logic, and the other part deals with the emotional aspect. Dr. Siegel and Dr. Payne-Bryson refer to the upstairs brain, which deals with reasoning and logic, and the downstairs brain, which is emotional. The emotional part of the brain reacts first, especially when a person is in an emotionally roused state.

As the brain develops, it begins to integrate the information between the emotional and logical sides. As this happens, a person reacts less intensely with emotions as he draws from the logical part of the brain. This process does not happen suddenly; it occurs gradually, through development and experience. This is where communication enters. Explaining to the child, at his level of understanding, helps the emotional and logical sides of the brain to connect, and the child begins to understand what is happening as he processes the event. As a parent (or involved adult) explains to the child, the child can begin to see the relationship of the behavior to certain consequences.

The emotional bond between parent and child is very deep, and a child is more likely to learn and absorb things from people they love and respect. As a child begins to understand the relationship between behavior and consequence, the relationship between parent and child is strengthened.

Power struggles can be avoided by looking beneath the behavior to discover the reason. The trigger for a behavior is not always obvious, and communication may help to uncover the source, helping people understand their feelings. When people are upset, they are emotionally dysregulated and cannot think clearly. This is why children need the nurturing of a parent or caregiver to reconnect, explain, and redirect. If you, as a parent or caregiver, are emotionally dysregulated and frustrated, take time to calm down so you can help the child regroup. No one is perfect, and as parents, we make many mistakes. We can learn from these mistakes, and this gives our children an opportunity to witness changing a negative situation into a positive learning experience. Validate the child's reality and address thoughts, feelings, and behavior.

Socialization and interactions within the family of origin become a foundation for the formation of social skills and future interactions. Family is the first of all social experiences, and from this environment children learn and experience their first interactions, which they continue to build on. Storytelling among the generations is a powerful connector, as children learn about older family members' life experiences, and younger ones share their own experiences and thoughts. Intergenerational relationships strengthen the bonds between family members. Subsequent generations may choose to follow similar patterns as previous generations did, or they may decide to change to patterns that are more appropriate for their circumstances.

There will always be sibling rivalry. Depending on the temperaments of the children involved, the rivalry may be overt, with bickering, fighting, and arguing. Or it may be more covert with a silent power struggle going on as each child tries to seek attention. That being acknowledged, it is important that the family is a team and functions as a team.

Both heredity and environment affect personality development (Toman 1976). Birth order has been the subject of psychological and social research, and proponents of birth order theories have asserted that children develop certain personality characteristics and interaction patterns in response to their family environment. The study of birth order's effect on the personality can be traced back to 1869, when Francis Galton reported that eminent scientists were often firstborn. In the twentieth century, Alfred Adler was one of the first to offer a comprehensive theory pertaining to birth order. He theorized that birth order affects lifestyle and development, and he believed certain characteristics are attributed to the birth order in the family of origin. Adler believed that the interaction patterns and coping skills developed in the family of origin are carried through life in the way people continue to interact, problem-solve, and cope. He also observed that people develop lifestyle patterns, and these patterns repeat themselves in family histories. It has been suggested that children may develop coping strategies that might exaggerate birth order effects, in response to parents or siblings.

Controversial studies have been conducted over the years in an attempt to identify the eldest as more intelligent as previously stated by Galton. Results from these studies correlating birth order with intelligence and achievement are ambiguous. Some research shows that firstborns achieve higher academics and attain leadership positions in their careers. Firstborns have been observed to be more responsible and more likely to conform to family values than later born siblings. Although conservative in their thinking and actions, firstborns can be power oriented.

Middle children have often been identified as peacemakers or negotiators; they have also been identified as more stubborn, less compliant, and more challenging than the firstborn. Younger siblings learn vicariously through older siblings as they observe experiences and consequences to behaviors. They have learned the way around the system, and last-born children often develop clever ways to get attention. They are good at reading people and are often more socially oriented.

Last-born children are often more people oriented than firstborns, who tend to be task oriented. Last-born children have been shown to be more open and accepting than firstborns or middle children. Studies have demonstrated that last-born children take a creative approach to management and may adopt a hands-off management style. They are often delegators. Youngest children may exhibit characteristics that can be developed in a positive way or serve to be detrimental. For example, youngest children are known to be more relaxed and have a good sense of humor. In a positive and relaxed approach, they may use humor in a positive way, promoting good interactions and good feelings, or they may use humor in a negative way acting like the class clown or the office jerk. I believe that family environment influences success of last-born children. For example, if the last-born is treated like a baby and autonomy is not encouraged, the last-born may be more dependent and less likely to accept responsibility appropriate for developmental levels. If they are accepted at their developmental level and given opportunities appropriate for that level, they will have a better chance of thriving and using their birth order characteristics in a positive way. Last-born children can be manipulative and charming, or they can learn to use their charm in a positive way. Social orientation attributed to the last-born can be cultivated into the ability to work well with people, helping others to develop to their own potential. Or the last-born could use social orientation to manipulate others for personal gain. An only child may display characteristics of both firstborn and last-born and even a middle child. The family environment strongly influences the further development of birth order characteristics.

Birth order characteristics remain throughout life. As people mature, they learn to improve strengths and adapt negative characteristics. Chronological birth order does not always determine birth order effects. Many variables can impact the degree of birth order effects, such as the gender and spacing of siblings, interaction of parents with each child and with each other, health and birth order of parents, socioeconomic status of the family, death of a family member, serious illness, separation of a sibling, divorce, or blended families. At times, role reversals may occur. A child may bond with a sibling who seems threatening.

Family dynamics change with the addition of each member. If more than five years exist between siblings, the eldest is less dependent on the primary caregiver and can function more independently in the world than a toddler. With five or more years between siblings, birth order characteristics tend to start over. If the second born of three children has disabilities or limitations, that child may take on the characteristic of the youngest child, and the third born adopts the characteristics of a middle child. Multiple interactions occur within each family environment, which can shape personality (Toman 1976).

In the case of twins, the birth order characteristics may differ. Identical twins, which are fertilized with one egg and one sperm that divide into two zygotes, will have more characteristics in common than fraternal twins. Identical twins will always be the same sex. As they originate from two eggs fertilized by two sperm, fraternal twins may be more like individual siblings rather than identical twins.

Walter Toman, who studied the effects of birth order in the twentieth century after Adler, stated, "A person's family represents the most influential context of a person's life than do any other life contexts" (Toman 1976, 5). "The effects of family influences are covert, and appear in sentiments and attitudes in basic wishes and interests of which the person may be partly unaware" (Toman 1976, 6). A nurturing environment promotes positive self-esteem, respect for each individual, and the development of self-awareness. Discipline is provided through positive guidance and establishment of developmentally appropriate limits and expectations, and it allows for individual growth and developmentally appropriate independence.

A family functions as a team in which all members participate. Parents set the tone. Planning fun activities together as a family strengthens bonds with cooperation. Fun activities may vary, depending on family and individual interests. Sometimes it may feel like life is overwhelming, but we need to search for the silver lining in the clouds that overtake us. If we search, we can usually find a learning experience somewhere among the trials. As we evolve, it is important to appreciate the uniqueness of each individual, remembering that we, as adults, evolve too. We have our own interests and should not live vicariously through our children or their successes.

The nature of families differs. A half century ago, a typical nuclear family in the United States consisted of two parents and a varied number of children. Today, there are many types of families. Whatever the family constellation, it is important to remember that each family is composed of individuals who are trying to work together, and solutions will vary depending on the needs.

Families are more mobile than fifty to one hundred years ago. It is common for grandparents to live a distance from grandchildren, but with modern technology, they can communicate easily across the miles. What is important is that the family, whatever the composition, is the main stabilizing and influential factor in children's lives. Grandparents and other family members who are involved contribute to the family environment, whether by Skype, FaceTime, texting, phone, letters, or physical presence. A nurturing environment encourages children to reach their potential and walk their journey to healthy interdependence.

Chapter 10

The Storms of Life

> Would to God these blessed calms would last. But the mingled, mingling threads of life are woven by warp and woof: Calms crossed by storms, a storm for every calm.
> —*Moby Dick*

Moby Dick was required reading for many of us in high school. As adolescents, did we comprehend many of the abstract meanings and their applications to life in *Moby Dick* or the other classics we were required to read? We may have moaned and groaned about having to read these books. We may have liked some parts, and there might have been class discussion that we listened to and participated in, but we didn't give the topic much deep thought afterward. As adults, with life experience, maybe we chose to reread some of these books and can more clearly see their implications.

Using the sea as a metaphor for life, Melville points out that the sea is not constantly calm and good; there are storms, and sometimes these storms are destructive. When they occur, the intensity with which they occur is out of our control. I have often pondered life's questions, and I recognize that the storms of life can occur suddenly, changing many things.

In our lives, there are many ups and downs, interspersed with storms. Some of these storms we anticipate, and others take us by surprise. As we sit atop a mountain, feeling happy and blessed with life's wonders, we enjoy happiness. We may feel euphoric, or peaceful and calm, free from stress and negativity. We want this feeling to last forever. But it does not last. Suddenly, we find ourselves sliding downward, leaving the mountaintop in spite of wanting to stay. We have lost control. The journey down may be slow, and we know it is happening but we can't stop the process. Or it may be thrust upon us suddenly, with little or no warning. We can't stop the fall, and as we land in a valley, we may feel low, frustrated, scared, depressed, anxious, angry, or any combination of those feelings. As we have heard before, there is a silver lining in every cloud, and sometimes we have to search to find that glimmer when life throws negative events at us. Maybe there is something we can do to lessen the pain and consequences of the negative. Eventually a positive wind comes our way, and we hold on to a positive goal, even though the outcome may be may be questionable. During this time, it helps to remember the positive and take one step at a time.

Resilience, the ability to cope and deal with life's challenges, varies among individuals. Some people seem to have more resilience than others. With resilience comes a more positive sense of self in solving problems and managing stress. When people with resiliency are knocked down by life's struggles, they seem to come back stronger. Why are some people more resilient than others? Is it in their nature? Or have they learned how to deal with the storms of life? Environment plays a vital part, as does a person's outlook on life. Studies have shown that a resilient person usually has at least one very supportive person encouraging, validating, and providing positive feedback. A supportive environment helps a person deal with challenges and utilize skills to move forward.

Research shows that the neurotransmitters in our brains can influence how we react to stress, and these neurotransmitters contribute to moods. The amount of endorphins, the feel-good chemical, varies in individuals. Studies have shown that some people have a genetic predisposition for resilience because more endorphins are released. Observations, including those by Erikson, Bateson, and Vaillant, have shown that positive attitudes, and the ability to be flexible and open to life's experiences, bring us to integrity and wisdom. Resilience can be prompted with self-reflection, through writing and discussion.

Remaining open to adapting as life presents challenges and using positive coping skills can be difficult, but we owe it to ourselves to try so that we are not defeated. This is part of self-care, or parenting ourselves. It may feel easier to not expend the energy, but just sit back and be miserable. Using coping skills requires effort and hard work, and sometimes we have to try several strategies before finding an effective one. There are many coping skills, which can be modified to meet an individual's needs. A coping skill that works for one person may not be effective for another. We might ask ourselves, "What can I do at this time when I feel life has taken a nasty turn for me? How do I cope with this unwanted change?" People have a choice: they can wallow in self-pity, or they can search for a glimpse of the positive. Adjusting to life's challenges and changes are difficult, and grieving may accompany a major change. Dr. Vaillant (2002) cited the coping mechanism of sublimation, applying one's passion to something new when we can no longer follow the previous passion. This is helpful when major changes present themselves, such as empty nests, retirement, a major loss, or significant changes in lifestyle. In that process, one may pass through the stages of grief for something lost, but positive skills can be used as part of self-care. Being open to receiving support from others, journaling, or self-expression in a positive way can help us.

None of us are immune to the storms of life, nor can we always predict them. There may have been a fear, maybe unacknowledged, in the back of our minds. Suddenly, the storm is thrust upon us, and we must cope. Storms affect not only the individual but also all those around the person. A family is affected when an individual suffers a physical illness, a serious injury, or an emotional setback or trauma. Friends, coworkers and those involved are impacted. Reactions vary and can include compassion, empathy, concern, or desire to help. Sadness and tears are a common response. The reactions of some people may be intense, and others may appear aloof. Aloofness may be due to fear of the future, fear of how the relationship may be affected, fear of how others will be impacted, fear of abandonment, or fear of not knowing how to respond. An appearance of aloofness or insensitivity is the outer layer of response, and true feelings may lie deep within the core of the person. Fear may be at an unconscious level. Denial is a common response, especially among family members and those close to the individual. It is helpful to remember people vary widely in their responses, especially in vulnerable moments.

A Personal Experience

Being diagnosed with cancer was a threat to my physical and emotional well being, impacting my quality of life, threatening my future plans, and interrupting my comfortable and predictable lifestyle. I asked all the questions: Why me? Why now? I didn't ask for this, so why? I try to live a healthy life, so why? What is my purpose in life? These are questions that anyone asks when confronted with a crisis. Although I had never verbalized my deep fear of cancer, it had always been there in the back of my mind. I think watching my father's health deteriorate from cancer when I was four years old may have been the beginning of that fear, and it was a contributing factor in my awareness that mortality can be fragile.

My symptoms presented as respiratory, with exacerbated asthma symptoms, which were a part of my medical history. I also experienced fatigue, which I passed off to age and a busy life. I was in denial at first, not fully acknowledging my symptoms. When symptoms did not improve with all the usual home treatment, I scheduled a visit with my physician.

I began going through the stages of grief. Suddenly, the seriousness was more realistic as I began further testing. I don't think I passed through denial until I heard the results of the biopsy. Then my thoughts turned to the fact that I had a blood cancer, as my father had. I had a different type of lymphoma than he did, but it was still a blood cancer. I asked myself, "What is all this? What is the genetic factor here?" Well, the genetic factor became even more prominent and concerning when, two and a half months after my diagnosis, my youngest daughter, age thirty-three, was diagnosed with acute lymphoblastic leukemia (ALL). *Why? What is going on? This feels unreal! Three generations in a row with blood cancers! What is the meaning of all this?* My mind was a jumble as I struggled with questions that seemed to have no answers—worries and fears that I could not predict the outcome of and I had no control over. I was an emotional wreck in my oncologist's office about five days after I learned of my daughter's diagnosis. With appropriate empathy and compassion, he assured me that as my treatment progressed, we would look for answers and outreach clinicians who might have information on the latest research in genetics and blood cancers. My oncologist arranged for a consultation with a physician who heads the research to identify a genetic link in blood cancers. I did not receive any definite answers, but at least I knew I was not far off base with my suspicions about a genetic involvement.

My daughter and I were so fortunate. Now, four years later, as I marvel at my good health and my daughter's good health, it all seems like a nightmare. The storm was intense and fearful, but we rode it out. How? Why? Will cancer ever recur or strike another family member? Will someone in the next generation be affected? We don't know the answers, but we can appreciate the gift of life each day.

Fear is a natural reaction when we experience threats to our health and we encounter life situations we can't control. Avoidance can sometimes accompany that fear. It might feel easier to avoid reality than deal with it. If we don't think about something, maybe it will go away. This was not going away, and I realized I had to stare this fear in the face and find ways to care for myself while also supporting my daughter and her family. I knew if I could be positive and calm, the rest of my family would fare better. I temporarily could not be the independent, active person I had always been. Wonderful friends and family members were there to support and help during this terrible storm. I gratefully accepted their help. My daughter and I were open and honest about our diagnoses, making it easier for others to support us.

Supernatural is the best word I can think of to describe my experience of passing through the grieving stages. Intellectually, I was aware of what was happening, and emotionally I was feeling all the pain. It felt like I was standing by, watching myself go through this process. As I seemed to pass out of denial, I realized I was extremely angry. How dare anyone or anything do this to my child? I bargained, I was depressed, and I was scared! Many times, I bargained with God to let my daughter be healthy, and if it was time for one of us to die, let it be me and not my Katie. Her family needed her; her boys were five and two and needed their mom. I had to learn to look for even the smallest positive sign.

When I discovered my daughter's diagnosis, I was a patient in a local hospital, being treated for a partially collapsed lung, a complication of my illness and treatment. She had been experiencing flu-like symptoms, and by Thursday, she realized her symptoms had worsened and she noticed her spleen was enlarged. She told me in a phone conversation she was returning to the doctor, and later she called to say the doctor had sent her to the emergency room for blood work, x-rays, and scans. I began to feel nervous, considering her enlarged spleen. Sometimes, being a nurse is an advantage, but it was *not* this time. She later called to report her mono test was negative, but her blood count was off, and she was being admitted to the hospital for observation and further assessment. A hematologist would be consulting. Thoughts of blood cancer raced through my head. I felt I knew at that time that she possibly had leukemia. There was nothing I could do. I couldn't see her. I couldn't be there with her to love her and protect her. I was stuck in the hospital as a patient. Early the following morning, my fears became a reality when she called and told me the diagnosis. She was going to be transported by ambulance from the local hospital to the oncology unit in a larger teaching hospital. I was not in critical condition, but I couldn't go anywhere. My doctors cautioned me to be off antibiotics and stable at home for several days before I traveled to see her. I had to rely on the reports of others. I couldn't see my daughter and assess her for myself. I was used to independence, and I felt I was losing it. I couldn't share my fears with Katie or my other two daughters. I wanted to scream, but knew I couldn't. I did share my concerns with appropriate people, because I knew it was not healthy for me to hold my feelings in. I cried a lot. Many wonderful friends, family members, and coworkers were there to give me love and support.

The days passed slowly, and I grasped at each positive thing I could find. I was stable, and my daughter responded immediately to the aggressive treatment. I clung to that. Finally, after a week, I was able to visit and see for myself how she was. It was a gift to be there with her for a few hours. In time, my health battle subsided, when after six months of chemotherapy, my PET scan was negative, showing no signs of the presence of cancer in my body. A huge relief, but I was exhausted and emotionally fragile after treatment. My daughter's treatment progressed over a period of more than two years. Her treatments lessened in intensity, and as she traveled the journey, there were some hospitalizations to address the side effects of medication. I began to feel less worried as she slowly gained energy. I marveled at how well she was able to take care of her family, and I focused on any positive sign, no matter how slight. Sometimes I felt as though it took more energy to remain focused on the positive, but I couldn't let myself go down the path of negativity. Self-care was important. In addition to the love and support of family and friends, I had to rely on myself to structure rest times, eat healthily, and nurture myself.

I knew I was experiencing the stages of grief, and sometimes it felt like I was an outsider, watching myself. I was angry, I bargained, I was depressed, and I soul searched.

How would I get through this? I realized I had a choice. I could be a victim, or I could try to be positive. It was a struggle. I made myself look for the positive, no matter how small; I tried to remain focused on the positive. It was difficult for me to adapt from my usual level of functioning to the decreased level I was at. I have always been a goal-oriented person who focuses on details, with plan A ahead. I've always gone with the philosophy that you have plan B ready to go if A doesn't work out. Now, I was adapting to plan C, D, or whatever. I set small, daily goals for myself. Every morning, I forced myself to make my bed, get dressed, and eat a small breakfast. Then I usually moved to the sofa, where I spent a good portion of my day. I planned small goals throughout the day; maybe a load of laundry, a few yoga poses or simple exercises, clean the kitchen, dust, or pay bills. I began to live one day at a time, one hour at a time, and sometimes minute by minute. I thought, *Okay, this moment is good. This is what I have to be thankful for right now.* Every morning when I awoke, I said to myself, "Okay. This is good. I am breathing. I am moving. And I am thinking. I will take one step at a time. This is good." I continue to do that every day. I was able to work part-time during my treatment, which helped me focus on something other than my worries.

Was I angry? Oh, yes, I was angry! I tried to express my anger, knowing it was not healthy to suppress it. I tried to avoid taking my anger and frustration out on other people because it was not their fault. I acknowledged that I was angry at circumstances. I was angry at the tumor, which had slowly grown on the mediastinum, between my two lungs, causing my right lung to fill with fluid. I was angry that the tumor was next to the aorta, posing even more of a risk. I expressed my anger at the tumor, and there were times that I yelled and screamed at the nasty tumor, telling it that I had not invited it into my body and therefore it had no right to be there. I used visual imagery and imagined the tumor shrinking away to nothing. I imagined the chemo drugs acting as an army of soldiers entering my body to kill the evil. I even visualized going into my body with my bare hands and ripping that blasted tumor out of my body. It sounds crazy, but that is what I did, reassuring myself those skills were helping me express my anger and grief in the right direction. Having those images of attacking the tumor gave me a sense of relief, and my anger lessened. Also, I felt anger at my father and grandparents for passing on the blood cancer gene. I knew it wasn't their fault, and they certainly had no way of knowing, but I felt the anger. In response to my anger, I placed my father's picture facedown in an end table drawer until I had resolved the anger and felt calmer.

I tried my best to support my daughter and her family. I tried to be strong and positive. I relished every positive sign in her recovery and every sign of strength. Again, I had to remind myself to take one step at a time. Reminding myself daily of our good fortune and returning health, I found myself wondering about the purpose in life, specifically my purpose. I believe my coping skills and positive attitude were key in my recovery. Was it easy? No! But I believe faith and a positive attitude are healing and can help overcome misery and pain, whether emotional or physical.

The journey of life requires continuous adapting if we are to weather the storms that are cast upon us through no fault of our own. Using coping skills can be a struggle that takes time and energy. One round of deep breathing does not make our anxiety, fear, or anger dissipate. It takes practice, practice, and practice. In the next paragraphs, I will suggest some coping skills that are effective for many people. Sometimes one skill doesn't work, so we try another skill. This is how we build resilience, and it is a slow process.

Acknowledging and Expressing Your Feelings

Anger, frustration, and anxiety, when not expressed, grow and spread, sometimes building into a volcano-like reaction. All emotions are okay, and it is how we express these emotions that is right or wrong. Whatever we feel needs to be recognized, while acknowledging appropriate ways to express that feeling. Everyone feels angry at some point. Feeling anger is okay; it is how you express the feeling that is acceptable or not acceptable.

Anxiety is another feeling shared by all of us, at one time or other. Letting anxiety overpower you can increase stress and contribute to frustration and a lower self-esteem, causing you to doubt yourself and your abilities. Yelling, screaming, swearing, or hurting other people with physical force or words is not acceptable. As role models, adults can guide children and teens to healthy forms of expression of emotions.

Deep Breathing

Deep breathing is a simple skill that is not as valued as it should be. Be still. Sit with your breath. Focus on your breath. Take a slow, deep breath in through your nose to the count of four; hold the breath for the count of four, then slowly exhale completely through either your mouth or nose. The number can vary. Some people count to three, others to five. Try to do a minimum of three deep breaths in a row.

The idea is to breathe oxygen into the body, and as the oxygen is inhaled deeply, the heart rate slows and steadies, blood pressure decreases, and the stress hormone, cortisol, is reduced. The body responds by relaxing. Placing one hand on your lower abdomen, you will feel the abdomen expanding slightly as you inhale and contracting as you exhale.

Known as diaphragmatic breathing, this skill is effective for decreasing anger, frustration, fear, worry, and anxiety, or when you need a minute to get calm and centered. Deep breathing releases endorphins, which act as a natural painkiller. The up-and-down motion of the diaphragm helps remove toxins from the organs.

I suggest not waiting until you are in a moment of anger or anxiety; practice this exercise on a regular basis. Try taking three deep breaths in this manner three times a day: once in the morning, once in the afternoon, and again before bedtime. Try to remember to use this skill whenever you feel anxiety, panic, fear, frustration, or anger. If you forget, do the breathing exercise after the fact. Don't just say, "Okay, I forgot to do it. I'll do it next time."

The more you practice, the more habitual it becomes. This exercise is also helpful for distracting your mind from pain, either physical or emotional. As you are focusing on your breath, visualize the body filling with calm, peaceful air, and then picture tension leaving the body with each exhalation.

Progressive Relaxation

Another helpful skill to decrease anxiety, fear, worry, anger, or frustration is progressive relaxation. Deep breathing along with progressive relaxation is very calming. Practicing this two-step activity teaches the body to relax when tense. The idea is to tense a group of muscles, and hold the group of muscles tense for the count of five, then relax. Notice how the muscles feel when tense and how they feel when relaxed.

Start with the feet and progress up both legs, tensing the muscles; then relax the leg and feet muscles. Next, tense the muscles in your arms, shoulders, chest, abdomen, and back, and then relax these muscles. Next, tense the muscles in your neck and skull—and then relax them. Do this with the entire body, tensing and relaxing several times. Stay in a relaxed state for fifteen seconds after each exercise. Over time, if practiced enough, the body will respond by automatically beginning to relax tense muscles. You can gradually tense and relax the entire body at the same time.

Notice what muscle groups you tend to tense with anxiety and anger. Pay attention to those muscles, practicing tensing and relaxing several times a day, even when not experiencing negative emotions. Practice checking in with your body to identify areas where you automatically tense your muscles. Some people clench their jaws. Relaxation and breathing are helpful in relieving the tension, as is massaging the jaw. Some people clench their fists; others tense different muscle groups in response to emotions, such as neck, upper back, and shoulders. Whatever your vulnerable area is, give it extra attention, focusing on this area when doing the progressive relaxation. Some people find the application of heat to these areas is helpful in relaxing the tense muscles. In reality, in many situations we can't apply heat, so continued practice of progressive relaxation is helpful.

Centering

Centering is a good tool for stress management. It is a technique you can use anywhere, anytime, and it is not necessarily noticeable to others unless they are attuned to it. Both feet should be placed flat and solidly on the floor, shoulder width apart. Close your eyes. Adjust your body to feel balanced. Focus on the center of your body, which is the central point of strength and balance, and visualize all your scattered energy being moved to the center of your body. This inner spot, in the abdomen, is your center of gravity. Visualize yourself being grounded, with your feet pushing into the earth. Visualize the here and now, the present. Push away all negative thoughts and outside pressures. Feel grounded. Focus on breathing.

Mindfulness

Mindfulness, paying attention to what you are doing in the present, also helps manage stress and decrease anxiety. Avoid thinking about the past or the future, which can raise anxiety levels. Be mindful of the present moment and maintain an accepting and nonjudgmental attitude. This seems difficult at first but becomes easier with practice and time.

Visual Imagery

Visual imagery can be powerful and is a way to express positive and happy things you wish for, as well as to lessen fear, anxiety, anger, and any other negative emotion. If you are feeling overwhelmed, sometimes it is helpful to imagine yourself on one side of a closed door, with many obstacles blocking access. Visualize slowly removing the things, one by one, and placing each one in a certain spot, knowing you will get to address it later but not all at once. Focus on one thing at a time. Break down the big tasks into smaller ones, and if you can visualize this happening, somehow it becomes easier to accomplish what you need to, and you feel calmer. Slowly, as each object falls into its place, the other side of the door seems less overwhelming, and you can open the door and venture to the other side. Picturing a door or obstacle and visualizing overcoming it can be helpful. Picture yourself as strong! This can work with a child or teen that is struggling with the multiple demands of life.

Visualize a happy place, a calm scene, or a funny incident; laughter is a good healer. I visualize clear water surrounded by green grass and beautiful flowers, with a blue sky on a warm sunny day. Some people identify a field, mountain, the ocean, or a flowing river as their calm place to retreat to in their minds.

Using Colors

Colors can symbolize emotions. Red can symbolize anger or energy. Blue is equivalent to calm, green to health, purple and violet to spirituality or a higher power, yellow to happiness and vibrant energy, and orange symbolizes energy.

Some people find it helpful to visualize colors to symbolize the mood they wish to achieve. Visualize healing colors and energy entering your body, forcing out the negative influences. Picture yourself as strong, healthy, and vibrant, radiating positive energy. Some colors help reduce symptoms of disease. (To digress, the word *disease* means to remove from comfort or ease. The prefix *dis* means not; with disease, something is wrong, and comfort is absent). Visualizing cannot hurt or interfere with a medical treatment, so if it works, why not practice it?

Self-Expression

Self-expression can bring about calmness, and there are many ways to do this. Journaling is one of the many ways to express thoughts and feelings. Reflecting on previous journal entries helps acknowledge accomplishments. It also is an opportunity to review a situation that was not handled in an appropriate and positive way. If time has passed since the event occurred, reviewing how it could have been handled differently promotes an understanding of the need to make changes. We all learn from our mistakes. Write and get your thoughts and feelings down on paper. I've always told kids that another good thing about journaling is that no one corrects your spelling. Just write and write.

Journaling thoughts and feelings can be done by drawing, which works for people with an inclination to draw or for young children. An exercise that is fun for children is to start a drawing with a line or circle and have the child add to it. Both of you keep adding spontaneously until you think you have a design. Then talk about the picture and what it looks like. Ask the child to tell a story about the picture, or the two of you work together on forming a story about the picture.

The following is a technique I employ is if a child has bad dreams or nightmares. I ask him to draw a picture of the scary part of the dream or the monster in the dream. After he tells me a little bit about it, I ask him to make multiple black marks and X's throughout the picture, a concrete act to imply the dream or monster is bad and not influential. Then I ask him, or together, we rip the paper into shreds and throw it in the trash. This serves as another symbol of ridding ourselves of the bad. Then we might talk about how he is bigger and stronger than the monster or the bad influence in the dream. We might draw a picture of the child as big and strong, able to be powerful over the monster, and then we visualize the child that way. Or the child can think about a more positive ending for the dream, talk about that ending, and maybe even draw a picture of it.

Another technique that works with anxiety is to have a child draw a picture of a shield, and then imagine the shield big and strong, made of invincible metal. We visualize placing the shield in front of him when anxiety or fear begins to mount. This takes practice, but many times it is helpful. Some kids choose to hang a picture of their shield somewhere in their home as a reminder of building strength.

Drawing, painting, sculpting, and other arts and crafts serve as therapeutic tools. Sculpting something out of clay or play dough is another form of self-expression. I know some art teachers who believe that anyone can paint as a form of self-expression; no talent is needed. Coloring has become a popular pastime and a calming activity for children and adults alike. One can invest in a fancy or simple coloring book, or draw pictures. Some children enjoy making their own book with a collection of their drawings and coloring. It is fun to listen to them create stories about their pictures.

Whatever works is what you do. If drawing or sculpting creates more stress, find another activity that feels more therapeutic. The important thing is that self-expression is helpful, and those feelings need to be released, not bottled up inside, building to a volcano.

Rating a feeling on a scale of one to ten helps us realize the intensity of an emotion, how the intensity changes, and its triggers. Observing the changes and relating them to skills that helped, or acts that worsened the intensity, helps identify when interventions are needed. For some people, it is helpful to draw or imagine a thermometer and then rate a feeling (sadness, anger, anxiety) on a scale of one to ten, with one being calm and ten being the highest. The person can identify a number (or numbers) on the scale where interventions are needed.

Music

Music is healing and calming for some people. Some people find listening to music can help them identify with a mood, so they choose music appropriate for that mood. If a person plays an instrument, playing helps to resolve negativity, allows expression, and brings about calm. Singing, whether or not a person has a "good voice," is helpful.

Empty Chair Technique

Sometimes there are things we wish we could have said to someone before they passed. At times, we wish we could speak our mind to another person, but it is not appropriate or healthy to do it at the time. These are the times when the empty chair technique can be effective. Pretend the person is sitting in a chair and express your thoughts and feelings. You can say whatever comes into your mind, and the person does not actually hear your anger or sadness, but you feel better because you have been able to express your thoughts and feelings. You are speaking from the heart and releasing emotions, whether they are positive ones or negative. Sometimes, if anger, frustration, or fear is the emotion you need to express, practicing it with the empty chair helps you find a way to express your emotions in an appropriate way. Writing a letter to a person but never mailing it is also effective. Expression is therapeutic in that you express what you wanted or needed to say, and you do not have to face a defensive person.

Listen to Your Body

Listen to your body. Your body appreciates a healthy lifestyle with exercise and healthy eating habits. Don't be upset if you venture off the healthy-food list sometimes; we all do. Relax and try attending to your mood when you tend to eat erratically or unhealthily.

Not only are exercise and motion beneficial for our physical and emotional health, they are healthy avenues to channel restlessness, frustration, and anger. Walking, running, swimming, yoga, tai chi—whatever works for you. Exercise releases endorphins and can alter our perspective. Dancing is an excellent form of exercise and self-expression. So is gymnastics, which has many similar postures as dancing.

Posturing, or placing one's body in a certain position, is helpful to some people in expressing emotions. Maybe regressing to a fetal position while crying is helpful. Taking an angry stance while deep breathing helps release anger. Sometimes if a person feels depressed, sitting in a slouched position wallowing in self-pity for a period of time helps. But do not feel this way for too long.

After expressing an emotion with posturing, turn

to a positive and helpful skill like breathing, progressive relaxation, or another activity that provides relaxation and enjoyment. I find light reading or watching a whimsical, light movie or television show promotes relaxation and calm and changes my perspective.

Sleep and Rest

Your body knows what it needs. Rest is an important part of maintaining health and energy. Sleep is healing, as the body and brain can rest and rejuvenate while you sleep. An identified rest period may not be feasible in a busy schedule, but you can take a few minutes when the opportunity arises to deep breathe, center, do progressive relaxation, or close your eyes and elevate your feet for a brief hiatus.

Get in the habit of following a good bedtime routine. No electronics for at least a half hour, or preferably an hour, before bedtime. Electronics stimulate brain activity, making it difficult to fall into a restful sleep.

Engage in a non-stimulating, relaxing activity before sleep. Reading is good, but choose something that is not intellectually stimulating or scary. Listen to relaxing music. If you tend to be a worrier and think you may wake in the middle of the night thinking about all that needs to be done the next day, make a list, establishing priorities, before you go to bed. Look at it after writing it, and remind yourself tomorrow is another day and you will accomplish what you can at that time. I find it helpful to keep paper and a pen on my nightstand, so I can write down last-minute thoughts. A warm shower or bath before bed is relaxing for some people.

Are You a List Maker?

Prioritize your to-do lists if you are a list maker. Do not be overly ambitious when you make your lists. Be realistic. I find it helpful to have a daily list, a weekly list, and an ongoing list. I love crossing things off as I accomplish them. Be aware that all the things on your tomorrow list may not be accomplished tomorrow and some can wait until the next day. Break large or overwhelming tasks into smaller tasks and accomplish a little at a time.

Remember that small, positive steps can accomplish just as much, if not more in the long run, than rushing headlong into an activity. Give yourself a break. Don't be hard on yourself if you don't accomplish as much as you would like. Small steps toward a goal are more satisfying than rushing and stressing. It can be hard to establish priorities, but it is worth it. Plan small rewards for yourself and include them in your schedule. Simple things like a cup of tea, a few minutes of reading something enjoyable, or sitting with closed eyes and feet elevated can provide respite. Tell yourself, after each small step, what you have done, and remind yourself that you are one step closer.

And remember, as adults, we are the role models. Experience emotions but try to remain positive. Research has shown that a person's attitude can affect healing. Practicing healthy outlets for emotions provides the younger generation with positive role models.

Bibliotherapy

Often our curiosity leads us to search for answers and solutions. We want to know the whys, how comes, and meanings. Searching for information through books, articles, or the Internet is referred to as bibliotherapy. Bibliotherapy, or research, has its place in providing possible solutions or answers and can lead to a different perspective or a new way of looking at things.

However, sometimes, too much research leads down the path of frustration as you have too much information, yet not enough. You need to know when to stop searching, and this can be difficult. At one point, before my diagnosis of lymphoma was confirmed, my daughter removed all medical books from my home, and I had to promise my physician and daughters I would not research on the Internet. This was difficult, as my mind always seeks information, but I forced myself to comply. Lighthearted television shows and movies provided a distraction for me, as did playing games of solitaire on my iPad.

Support and Validation

The importance of love and support cannot be overestimated. Identify the people who are your strongest supporters. They may be family members and friends. They may be coworkers. Appreciate their love and support. Reach out to your support persons. They will not know what you need unless you tell them what is going on with you.

If you are used to being independent, it can be difficult to accept help. If someone asks you what you need, state your needs. When they validate you, hear it and accept it gratefully. Support groups offer strength and unity, as everyone is struggling with the same or similar stressful challenges. Often, people will accept suggestions from someone who is dealing with the same challenges and emotions. If there are certain people who create stress and negativity, give yourself permission to avoid engaging with these people too often. You may have to interact with them sometimes, but you can respectfully avoid spending prolonged time with them.

Healthy Regression and Fantasy Are Not Only for Children

It may seem that children have an advantage because they can use play as a way to express themselves. Playing with a dollhouse and arranging furniture while pretending the doll family is engaging in an activity is something we often see children do. It is okay for adults too. Remember, at times we all regress, and it is okay if it does not impact functioning. If a mom wants to take a short break and arrange furniture in a dollhouse while she visualizes something, whether it is a dream, fantasy, or a sad event, it is okay. But if she spends most of her waking time playing with the dollhouse and neglects her needs and the needs of her children, this is an unhealthy point of regression.

All this takes energy. Yes, you will get tired. Small doses. Rest. Revive. Reward. Acknowledge your accomplishments. Write them down. Write one positive thing or accomplishment daily. Be thankful for each day and what you have, however small it may seem.

Chapter 11

The Evolving Wisdom of Parenthood

Children are not born with instruction manuals, and we don't receive periodic updates advising us of the next developmental stage and associated behaviors. Nor do we receive an informational describing the norms and variations within the norms. I think it is good that stereotyped manuals and updates are not available, for how could they adequately address the uniqueness of each child and individual temperament? There are many parenting books and self-help books, and sometimes the messages can be conflicting. Depending on the era in which they were written and the author's beliefs and mode of practice, styles differ. Some parenting suggestions may feel too rigid, others too flexible and open. Some may seem outdated, others too contemporary for someone's thinking and lifestyle. Some may be in conflict with a person's beliefs or values.

Ethics and morals begin in the family of origin. Whether

or not we choose to follow the same guidelines our parents did, the foundation has been laid, providing a base off of which we can make comparisons and decisions. There is no doubt that family systems have changed considerably in the last fifty years, and the constellation of a family plays a part in determining choices in parenting styles. In my years of searching and reviewing, I have found that what works best for me is to read and review information I think will be informative and helpful and then consider the pros and cons of different suggestions and styles. I look at what feels right, what I am most comfortable with, and what is appropriate considering the times. Then I make my decision. One can't gain insight and knowledge into parenting and development without becoming informed. Information received, processed, and reflected on offers the opportunity to choose the best styles of parenting and communication that fit in our world.

Remembering that our moral and ethical foundations were laid in our early development, and our first social experiences occurred within our family of origin, we have a beginning point for understanding our parents and realizing their perspectives at the time. Maybe we see something we really admire and choose to follow through with those patterns. Maybe we feel there is something that we were not comfortable with, and on reflection, we can find a different path that feels more comfortable for us, and our family.

The dynamics of a family are made up of the individual personalities, each one adding to the mixture. This is why two families may appear the same on the outside but have different dynamics and relationships on the inside. Previous studies of family systems have provided information on family structure and functioning. There is no such thing as the perfect family. The perfect family does not exist any more than the perfect person or the perfect relationship exists. In the best of situations, family members come together with their individual perspectives and work together to form a team. They work together to resolve differences and conflicts and create a workable common ground. Adults, especially parents and caregivers, are the ones who provide guidance and direction, and guidance can prove more beneficial with an understanding of development and its variations. In exploring resources for ways to improve family communication, a health care provider is a good place to start. School guidance counselors may be able to suggest resources as well.

Autocratic, permissive, and authoritative are the three styles of parenting that have been identified, over the last few decades, by various people and/or agencies. Pros and cons of these styles have been debated, and authoritative seems to come out on top. Autocratic parenting provides a dictatorship environment, with adults in complete control, sometimes even to the point of setting standards for personal beliefs and emotions. There is limited freedom to reflect, process, question, or choose. Discipline is in the realm of punishment and is often harsh. The permissive parenting style moves to the other end of the spectrum, allowing children too much freedom and setting too few limits. Discipline in the form of guiding and teaching is lacking. Parents may try to be their child's friend. This does not work. Adults have the experience to teach and guide and should not function as their child's equal. The authoritative style of parenting allows room for growth of all individuals. Children are given freedom but are expected to comply with safe and appropriate limits. Decisions, responsibility, and independence are gradually increased as children prove they are capable of accepting these privileges. Parents and caregivers discuss and explain as appropriate and only at a level the child can understand at that point. Love, support, respect, firm and consistent yet flexible limits, logical consequences, and mutual problem-solving among family members as appropriate—these offer an environment that promotes growth.

We don't necessarily think about ethics on a daily basis, but it is a part of our daily lives. Our morals, or personal ethics, guide the way we interact with others on a daily basis. The principles found in professional codes of ethics—integrity, dignity, respect, autonomy, beneficence, and do no harm—are an important part of our personal and interpersonal ethics as we live our lives. These principles most definitely apply to interpersonal ethics on a daily basis through interactions with children as well as peers.

As parents, caregivers, and mentors of children and youth, we set the stage. Although we provide the environment that nurtures success, we cannot live vicariously through our children. Our children's successes are their successes, and their shortcomings are theirs to work with, though we add our guidance and support. When our children succeed, we can pat ourselves on the back and say, "Good job," but the success is theirs, from their work and commitment. We can acknowledge that the support and environment we provided helped them reach success. As parents of adult children, we also realize that if our adult children make mistakes, they are the ones who actually made the choices. It is hard to sit and watch your adult children make mistakes or suffer hurt, whether emotional or physical. Over the years, people have been too quick to blame the negative choices of adolescents and young adults on the parents. We may feel disappointment and hurt when our adult children do things differently than we do, but it is important to remember that we did the best we could at the time, and we provided a foundation, which they used to make their decisions.

Joseph Campbell is well known for his statement, "Follow your bliss" (*The Power of Myth* 1988). While we are following our bliss, our own path, it is important to be cognizant of the paths our children are following. The paths may be similar or completely different, but they are separate journeys. While the paths may cross, we are all individuals.

Generations build on previous generations. Each generation meets new challenges, and through the new generation's eyes, the view of the world changes. Progress, setbacks, and challenges will continue to face us as the cycle of life evolves. It is important to draw on previous generations' knowledge and experience in problem solving while acknowledging present times. Intergenerational approaches to meet challenges can be invaluable, with components of wisdom and novelty. Drawing on the input of different generations and working together can be applied within the family unit, the community, a country, or culture.

A prime example is schools and families working together to nurture the next generations.

Alfred Adler asserted that life is a continuous process with continuity of past, present, and future, and there is always a part of the past and our foundation within us. A humanistic growth model, Adler's theory also professes that people can change and grow with encouragement. This falls into the realm of parenting, mentoring, or caregiving. Courage, support, and respect not only promote growth, but they are part of our interpersonal ethic (Dreikurs 1953; Hjelle and Zeigler 1992; Toman 1976). Erikson and Adler were near the beginning of a long line of people, both professional and lay, to acknowledge the importance of a balance between work and play, which can be translated into a balance for a parent between family, self, and employment.

The past and our recollections influence our present and impact our decisions. While acknowledging the impact the past might have played, it is important to maintain our present perspective and focus on the here and now. We all move through our lives with baggage. The challenge is to cope with how it impacts us in present day. We can look for the positive, practice tolerance, and acknowledge gratitude for our assets. We can all take steps for self-growth. Personal baggage can impact our relationships with family members, friends, and coworkers. Acknowledging and understanding the uniqueness in others is important, even if it is not in harmony with our own thinking. It is nonetheless important to realize that none of us can change another person. A person's behavior may change in response to our behaviors, but each person is an individual with an individual perspective. We can provide a nurturing environment, conducive to changes, but ultimately accept an individual for where they are now.

"Synchronicity" and "coincidences" are spoken of often today. Some people don't believe in coincidences, yet synchronous things happen all around us. At the time, we may not pay particular attention to coincidences as they occur, but on reflection, we may see an explanation. Why did this event happen at exactly this time? Why did I run into a certain person at a certain time? As we reflect on these occurrences, we may notice that things suddenly jump out at us at the right time, maybe offering us guidance. Coincidences often lead to new growth and understanding. When I was involved in a genealogy project for graduate school, I noticed many common themes among generations. Among the themes I observed were career choices, personality characteristics, and repetition of names among the generations where there was not a direct connection, like a junior, or obvious namesake. I also noticed a trend of common birth and death dates among a few family members. It fascinated me.

Just as there have been theorists on human development, there have been theorists who have identified career development and career choices. Some of these theories offer support to my belief that parenting can be considered a career. Donald Super, known for his work in vocational guidance and counseling, acknowledged career development as a progressive, developmental, step-by-step process throughout the life span. Parenting, in comparison, is a progressive, step-by-step process that continues through the life span. Super's theory also acknowledged that in a lifetime, a person's career is composed of stages of growth, exploration, establishment, maintenance, and decline, with specific tasks accomplished at each stage. This parallels the career of parenting, with the ups and downs, the frustrations countered with the times of pride and contentment. It also parallels human development and growth.

Super's theory followed the thoughts of Eli Ginzberg and Ann Roe, who in the 1950s acknowledged that early-childhood experiences play a part in influencing a person's career choices. Roe's work inspired further research on the early-childhood experiences influencing career choices. It must be recognized that the accuracy of childhood memories is also influenced by family retellings. The work of these researchers continues today, as career development holds an important place in the overall development of a person. As parents, teachers, caregivers, and mentors, we endeavor to provide an environment that nurtures strengths and talents and provides guidance and accommodations to remediate weaknesses? The challenges of parenting are to meet children at the developmental stage they are in at a given time, while acknowledging the integration of physical, emotional, cognitive, speech-language, spiritual, social, and ethical domains.

Hopefully, in helping parents and caregivers to understand the developmental process, child abuse and neglect can be eliminated as we work to promote optimal individual development in future generations. Knowledge and understanding of developmental stages can promote positive communication skills between the generations and provide an environment that promotes autonomy, creativity, and initiative. Learning is a continual process, and we are never too old to learn something new. We should remain open to the idea that each negative event offers a challenge and purpose for growth.

In understanding the developmental process through the life span, it is important to remember that we all need to belong and that much of our behavior stems from that need. We all need a source of meaning and fulfillment. We all need purpose, as purpose helps us to stay motivated. Having a purpose helps us stay energized and has health benefits. It's important to remember that negative emotions impact us, and impact our behavior, as do positive emotions, particularly in our interactions with our children. Intergenerational storytelling needs to continue, as it provides children with knowledge of past generations and different ways of thinking.

We have come a long way in understanding human development and how to provide nurturing environments. Through the years, we have added to and refined the developmental theories laid by Freud, Erikson, Bandura, Adler, Jung, Maslow, and others. New observations and research have led to changes in approaches, and we continue to learn. What we offer our children influences the future. As I neared completion of my first draft of this book, Dr. T. Berry Brazelton passed on. His research, observations, and work with families provided gentle guidance and education regarding development of infants and young children, especially the emotional and social aspects. His tireless devotion to helping parents in their journeys influenced more than one generation. His contributions to understanding the complex world of infants and young children have been significant and will be useful in the future. Many sources contribute to our understanding of the development of those we parent. These sources include practice, trial and error, observation, and research.

The journey of life continues, with twists and turns, as we move from one developmental stage to the next. Throughout this journey, we learn from our experiences and our interactions with others. Some of these experiences are memorable because of the positive feelings accompanying them. At times, unexpected storms may arise, knocking us off our path. These storms, although difficult and challenging to endure, add to our life experiences. When storms come, we may feel unequipped to face them, but as we move through the experience, we may be surprised at our strengths. Strength and experience gained through the storm provide us with valuable tools we can use to guide and support others. Wisdom is not reached with chronological age but comes when we can weave our experience with judgment, tolerance, and acceptance. With confidence in ourselves, and our beliefs, we should remain open to understanding the views of others as we nurture them. A wise person may have an opinion, continues to learn, and will adapt to necessary changes. The wise person is willing to problem-solve, and although a solution may not be near, the wise person listens and may offer suggestions to find an answer.

Dr. Vaillant, in *Aging Well* (2002), reminds that Erikson suggests that one of the life tasks of integrity is for the old to show the young how not to fear death. Dr. Vaillant quotes Henri Amiel, who in 1874 stated, "To know how to grow old is the master-work of wisdom, and one of the most difficult chapters in the great art of living" (Vaillant 2002, 59). This is true today as we contemplate the secret of successful aging. We gain insight and better understand development as we travel the journey.

Bibliography

American Heritage Dictionary. 2nd edition. 1982. Boston, MA: Houghton Mifflin.

American Academy of Pediatrics. 1991. *Caring for Your Baby and Young Child—Birth to Age 5.* New York: Bantam Books.

American Academy of Pediatrics. 1991. *Caring for Your School-Aged Child—Ages 5–12.* New York: Bantam Books.

American Academy of Pediatrics. 1991. *Caring for Your Adolescent—Ages 12–21.* New York: Bantam Books.

American Academy of Pediatrics. 2016. *Media and Children Communication Toolkit.* Retrieved April 2017. https://www.aap.org.

American Psychological Association Dictionary. 2017. www.apa.org.

Anmodt, S. 2011. "Brain Maturity Extends Well beyond Teen Years." N.H. Public Radio Broadcast. Retrieved August 2017. https://www.npr.org.

Aron, Elizabeth N., PhD. 2015. *The Highly Sensitive Child.* New York: Random House.

Attig, Thomas. 1996. *How We Grieve.* Oxford, England: Oxford University Press.

Barger, R., PhD. 2000. "A Summary of Lawrence Kohlberg's Stages of Moral Development." Notre Dame, IN: University of Notre Dame. Retrieved June 2017 from https://www.ccsudh.edu/dearhabermas. https://www.education.com/reference/article/kohlberg-moralreasoning.

Bateson, Mary Catherine. 2011. *Composing a Further Life: The Age of Active Wisdom.* New York: Random House.

Brazelton, T. Berry, MD. 1992. *Touchpoints.* Boston: Addison-Wesley Publishing Co.

Brazelton, T. Berry, MD. 2001. *Touchpoints: Three to Six.* New York: Perseus Publishing.

Brazelton, T. Berry, MD. 1984. *To Listen to a Child.* Boston: Addison-Wesley Publishing Co.

Britannica Encyclopedia. 2007. Chicago: Wikipedia. Retrieved May 2017.

Britannica Kids Dictionary. 2017. Retrieved May 2017. www.britannicakids.com.

Brooks, Robert, PhD, and Sam Goldstein, PhD. 2001. *Raising Resilient Children.* New York: McGraw-Hill Books.

Campbell, Joseph. 1988. *The Power of Myth.* New York: Doubleday Publishing Co.

Chapman, Gary, PhD, and Ross Campbell, MD. 2012. *The 5 Love Languages of Children.* Chicago: Northfield Publishing.

Cherry, K. 2017. "Preoperational Stage of Cognitive Development." Retrieved May 2017. https://www.verywell.com.

Corey, Gerald. 1996. *The Theory and Practice of Counseling and Psychotherapy.* 5th edition. Grove, CA: Brooks/Cole Publishing Co.

Cratty, B. J. 1971. *Active Learning.* New York: Prentice-Hall, Inc.

Crary, E. 1979. *Without Spanking or Punishment.* Seattle: Parenting Press.

Darling, N. 2016. *Social Learning Theory.* Retrieved April 2017. https://www.psychologytoday.com/basics/social-learning-theory.

Dinkmeyer, Don, James Dinkmeyer, and Gary McKay. 1989. *Parenting Young Children.* Minneapolis: American Guidance Service, University of MN.

Dobson, James. 1981. *The Strong-Willed Child.* Wheaton, IL: Tyndale Publishing.

Dodson, Fitzhugh, PhD. 1979. *How to Parent.* New York: Signet Books.

Dodson, Fitzhugh, PhD. 1979. *How to Discipline with Love.* New York: Signet Books.

Dreikurs, Rudolf, MD. 1953. *Fundamentals of Adlerian Psychology.* 5th edition. Chicago: Alfred Adler Institute.

Erikson, Erik. 1982. *The Life Cycle Completed. A Review.* New York: Norton & Co.

Erikson, Erik. 1963. *Childhood & Society.* 2nd revised edition. New York: Norton.

Forer, Lucille, PhD. 1976. *The Birth Order Factor: How Your Personality Is Influenced by Your Place in the Family.* New York: McKay Co.

Gesell, A., and F. Ilg. 1955. *The Gesell Institute's Child Behavior from Birth to 10.* New York: Harper & Row.

Gilligan, Carol. 1982. *In a Different Voice.* Cambridge: Harvard University Press.

Gilligan, Carol. 1988. *Mapping the Moral Domain.* Cambridge: Harvard University Press.

Ginot, Hiam. 1961. *Between Parent and Child.* New York: McGraw-Hill.

Hjelle, Larry, and Daniel Zeigler. 1992. *Personality Theories: Basic Assumptions, Research, and Applications.* 3rd edition. New York: McGraw-Hill.

Holly, James. 2014. "Your Life and Your Health." Retrieved January 2018. http://www.set.ma.com.

Holt, J. 1989. *Learning All the Time.* Boston: Addison-Wesley Publishing Co.

Horst, Elizabeth A. 1995. "Reexamining Gender Issues in Erikson's Stages of Identity and Intimacy." *Journal of Counseling and Development* 73 (January/February): 271–277.

"Infant Mental Health." 2016. Retrieved April 2017. https://www.waimh.org/i4.

Kubler-Ross, E., and D. Kessler. 2017. *Five Stages of Grief.* Retrieved July 2017. www.grief.the-five-stages-of-grief.com.

McDevitt, T. M., and J. E. Ormond-Pearson. 2010. "Kohlberg's Three Levels and Six Stages of Moral Reasoning." In *Child Development and Education*, p. 518. Retrieved June 2017. https://www.education.com/reference/article/kohlberg'smoralreasoning.

McLeod, S. 2010. "Concrete-operational Development." Retrieved May 2017. https://www.simplypsychology.org.

Marjoribanks, Kevin. 1990. "Sibling Variables: Correlates of Children's Academic Achievement." *Psychological Reports* 67: 147–154.

Mearns, J. 1989. "The Social Learning Theory of Julian B. Rotter." *American Psychologist* 44 (4): 625–626. Retrieved April 2017. https://www.en.wikipedia.org/wiki/Julian_Rotter.

Melville, Herman. 1851. *Moby Dick.* New York: Harper Publishing.

Merriam-Webster Dictionary. 2017. Retrieved May 2107. www.merriam-websterdicitonary.com.

Miller, Jean Baker. 1986. *Toward a New Psychology of Women.* Second edition. Boston: Beacon Press.

Mulac, M. E. 1987. *Educational Games for Fun.* New York: Harper & Row.

Munson-Miller, L. 1993. "Sibling Status Effect: Parent's Perceptions of Their Own Children." *Journal of Genetics Psychology* 154 (23): 189–198.

Newton, Lisa, ed. *Ethics in America.* 1989. New York: Corporation for Public Broadcasting and Columbia University Seminars.

"N.H. Infant Mental Health." 2017. Retrieved April 2017. https://www.nhimh.org.

Nolte, Dorothy Law. 1998. *Children Learn What They Live: Parenting to Inspire Values.* New York: Workman Publishing.

Oxford-English Dictionary. 2016. Retrieved May 2017. www.oxford-englishdictionary.com.

Piaget, J. 1954. "The Child's Conception of Numbers." *Journal of Consulting Psychology* 18 (1): 76.

Pipher, Mary, PhD. 1996. *The Shelter of Each Other: Rebuilding Our Families.* New York: Ballantine Books.

Ponzetti, James, ed. 2016. *Evidence-Based Parenting Education.* London, England: Routledge Publishing.

Redfield, James. 1993. *The Celestine Prophecy.* New York: Time Warner Books.

Redfield, James, and Carol Adrienne. 1995. *The Celestine Prophecy: An Experiential Guide.* New York: Time Warner Books.

Rykman, Richard. 1993. *Theories of Personality.* 5th edition. Grove, CA: Brooks/Cole Publishing Co.

St. Claire, Michael. 1989. *Object Relations Theory.* Grove, CA: Brooks/Cole Publishing Co.

Schab, Lisa M., LICSW. 2008. *The Anxiety Workbook for Teens.* Oakland, CA: Harbinger Books.

Schab, Lisa M., LICSW. 2009. *The Depression Workbook for Teens.* Oakland, CA: Harbinger Books.

Schell, Robert, and Elizabeth Hall. 1979. *Developmental Psychology Today.* 3rd edition. New York: Random House.

Schmitt, Barton, MD. 1987. *Your Child's Health.* New York: Bantam Books.

SHARE. 2015. National Headquarters in Missouri. Retrieved July 2017. https://info@nationalshare.org.

Sheedy, Mary. 1991. *Raising Your Spirited Child.* New York: Harper-Collins.

Siegel, Daniel, MD, and Tina Payne Bryson, PhD. 2014. *No-Drama Discipline.* New York: Random House.

Siegel, Daniel, MD, and Tina Payne Bryson, PhD. 2011. *The Whole-Brain Child.* New York: Random House.

Small, Gary, MD. 2008. *Surviving the Technological Alteration of the Modern Mind: The i brain.* New York: Harper-Collins Publishing.

Toman, Walter, PhD. 1976. *Family Constellations.* New York: Springer Publishing Co.

Vaillant, George, MD. 2002. *Aging Well.* New York: Hachette Book Co.

Watts, Sherry K., Tracy L. Robinson, and Helen Lupton-Smith. 2002. "Building Ego and Racial Identity." *Journal of Counseling and Development* 80 (Winter): 94–100.

White, Burton, PhD. 1975. *The First Three Years of Life.* New York: Avon Publishers.

White, Burton, PhD. 1995. *The First Three Years of Life.* Revised. New York: Simon & Schuster.

White, B. 1995. *The First Three Years of Life.* Revised. Retrieved April 2017. http://www.theallianceforcec.org/library.

Zunker, Vernon. 1994. *Career Counseling and Applied Concepts of Life.* Grove, CA: Brooks/Cole Publishing Co.

Interesting Reading for Parents

American Academy of Pediatrics. 1991. *Caring for Your Baby and Young Child—Birth to Age 5*. New York: Bantam Books.

American Academy of Pediatrics. 1991. *Caring for Your School-Aged Child—Ages 5–12*. New York: Bantam Books.

American Academy of Pediatrics. 1991. *Caring for Your Adolescent—Ages 12–21*. New York: Bantam Books.

American Academy of Pediatrics. 2016. *Media and Children Communication Toolkit*. Retrieved April 2017. https://www.aap.org.

Aron, Elizabeth N., PhD. 2015. *The Highly Sensitive Child*. New York: Random House.

Bateson, Mary Catherine. 2011. *Composing a Further Life: The Age of Active Wisdom*. New York: Random House.

Brazelton, T. Berry, MD. 1992. *Touchpoints*. Boston: Addison-Wesley Publishing Co.

Brazelton, T. Berry, MD. 2001. *Touchpoints: Three to Six*. New York: Perseus Publishing.

Brazelton, T. Berry, MD. 1984. *To Listen to a Child*. Boston: Addison-Wesley Publishing Co.

Brooks, Robert, PhD, and Sam Goldstein, PhD. 2001. *Raising Resilient Children*. New York: McGraw-Hill Books.

Chapman, Gary, PhD, and Ross Campbell, MD. 2012. *The 5 Love Languages of Children*. Chicago: Northfield Publishing.

Cratty, B. J. 1971. *Active Learning*. New York: Prentice-Hall, Inc.

Crary, E. 1979. *Without Spanking or Punishment*. Seattle: Parenting Press.

Dobson, James. 1981. *The Strong-Willed Child*. Wheaton, IL: Tyndale Publishing.

Dodson, Fitzhugh, PhD. 1979. *How to Parent*. New York: Signet Books.

Dodson, Fitzhugh, PhD. 1979. *How to Discipline with Love*. New York: Signet Books.

Forer, Lucille, PhD. 1976. *The Birth Order Factor: How Your Personality Is Influenced by Your Place in the Family*. New York: McKay Co.

Gesell, A., and F. Ilg. 1955. *The Gesell Institute's Child Behavior from Birth to 10*. New York: Harper & Row.

Ginot, Hiam. 1961. *Between Parent and Child*. New York: McGraw-Hill.

Holly, James. 2014. "Your Life and Your Health." Retrieved January 2018. http://www.set.ma.com.

Holt, J. 1989. *Learning All the Time*. Boston: Addison-Wesley Publishing Co.

Mulac, M. E. 1987. *Educational Games for Fun*. New York: Harper & Row.

Nolte, Dorothy Law. 1998. *Children Learn What They Live: Parenting to Inspire Values.* New York: Workman Publishing.

Pipher, Mary, PhD. 1996. *The Shelter of Each Other: Rebuilding Our Families.* New York: Ballantine Books.

Redfield, James. 1993. *The Celestine Prophecy.* New York: Time Warner Books.

Redfield, James, and Carol Adrienne. 1995. *The Celestine Prophecy: An Experiential Guide.* New York: Time Warner Books.

Schab, Lisa M., LICSW. 2008. *The Anxiety Workbook for Teens.* Oakland, CA: Harbinger Books.

Schab, Lisa M., LICSW. 2009. *The Depression Workbook for Teens.* Oakland, CA: Harbinger Books.

Schmitt, Barton, MD. 1987. *Your Child's Health.* New York: Bantam Books

Sheedy, Mary. 1991. *Raising Your Spirited Child.* New York: Harper-Collins.

Siegel, Daniel, MD, and Tina Payne Bryson, PhD. 2014. *No-Drama Discipline.* New York: Random House.

Siegel, Daniel, MD, and Tina Payne Bryson, PhD. 2011. *The Whole-Brain Child.* New York: Random House.

Vaillant, George, MD. 2002. *Aging Well.* New York: Hachette Book Co.

White, Burton, PhD. 1995. *The First Three Years of Life.* Revised. New York: Simon & Schuster.

White, B. 1995. *The First Three Years of Life.* Revised. Retrieved April 2017. http://www.theallianceforcec.org/library

Index

Information on the developmental theories of Erikson, Kohlberg, Piaget, and other theorists can be found in chapter 1. Information relating to different developmental stages through the lifespan can be found in chapters corresponding to life stages. For example, information on infant development will be found in chapter 2, entitled *"Infancy: Getting to Know Each Other."* Information pertaining to adolescents will be found in chapter 6, *"Adolescence: The Struggle of Identity"*, and information on adult development can be found in chapter 7, *"Adulthood: Continuing the Journey"*. Information on communication skills can be found in several chapters. Discipline is mentioned in several chapters, according to stages.

A